8/
8 5

# SOCIAL WORK STRESS AND INTERVENTION

# Social Work Stress and Intervention

STEPHEN FINEMAN
*Senior Lecturer in Organizational Behaviour,*
*School of Management,*
*University of Bath*

Gower

Published by
Gower Publishing Company Limited,
Gower House, Croft Road, Aldershot, Hants GU11 3HR,
England

and

Gower Publishing Company,
Old Post Road, Brookfield, Vermont 05036, USA.

British Library Cataloguing in Publication Data

Fineman, Stephen
   Social work stress and intervention.
   1. Social workers——Great Britain——Job stress
   I. Title
   361.3'2019      HV245

   ISBN 0-566-00664-2


Printed and Bound in Great Britain by
Biddles Limited Guildford and Kings Lynn

# Contents

My thanks to Iain Mangham, Judi Marshall, Mike Campbell and Rona Fineman for their comments on earlier drafts of this book. I am indebted to Joan Budge for her efforts in the preparation of the manuscript.

# Preface

This book describes a study of the stresses and organisational experiences of five teams of social workers. It also charts my influences, as a helper, working with them.

A director of a local authority social services department in the United Kingdom was anxious to 'do something about the high level of stress amongst some fieldwork and related staff'. He approached me, knowing of my own professional interest in stress. For his part, almost any form of help would have his blessing, although he was more than wary about a classical social science study involving what he saw as the paraphernalia of pre-structured tests and questionnaires, large prescribed samples, modest interaction with staff, and an unwieldy report to him at some indeterminate future date. It became apparent that his caution and scepticism were not unreasonably based as a number of grand studies had been conducted in his organisation which had left seemingly little that was helpful, and a lot of consumer resistance to 'being studied'.

For my part, the Director's concerns provided an exciting challenge to develop features of 'intervention' research into stress which had already occupied me, as an organisational psychologist, for some time. While there has been a proliferation of research into stress in recent years, especially in the traditional streams of psychology and sociology, rarely has direct help for the subjects of research been an intrinsic and immediate purpose of such study. Yet the relative intimacy of the helping relationship provides fertile ground for gathering sensitive perceptions which may otherwise be closed to the more distant, 'uninvolved' researcher, data appropriate for research discovery, client self-discovery, and planned action to relieve stress.

The present investigation represents my attempt to put this philosophy into practice in the study of social worker stress: to fuse the researcher and helper roles such that one might enrich the other. It is also a way of thinking which helps me to smooth some ethical wrinkles about researching troubled people: they are potentially direct bene-ficiaries of a process in which they, and I, elect to participate. They are not simply performing 'specimens' for my observations.

This book contains what I found out from this approach. It details social workers' problems and stresses, such as the effects of their own institu-tionalisation - office and organisational politics; how they strive to create meaning and purpose in situations where they are unsure of what they are doing, and why they are doing it; coping with multiple emotional demands - and failing to cope. All this is revealed through the window of a counselling process where I am the counsellor looking in, and also participating in their problems and experiences.

The study ultimately, and intimately, involved 40 people, mainly fieldworkers. For them, the experi-ence was a very unusual one: professional helpers, it seems, rarely seek professional help. Hopefully this account provides some illuminating perspectives from my two years work with them. Not only about the nature of their stresses, but also about my own role as a helper. I have tried hard to guard confi-dentiality in my reporting. All participants are disguised and I do, in the main, discuss illustra-tive themes.

The book is structured in four parts. Part I describes the background and rationale to the study.

Part II is devoted to an analysis of the social workers' perceptions of stress. In Part III the counselling process is examined in detail, as it was central to both helping the social workers and generating the research data. The final part provides a broader base from which to examine the results of the study, and I offer some speculations on the implications of the findings for social worker stress and help.

# Part I
# Context and method

# 1 The study setting

The study took place in one of five major regional areas of an English local authority social services department (see Figure 1.1). It was the most densely populated region - a predominantly urban one of some 200,000 population. The region's town was founded upon a now declining engineering industry, but it was making some progress towards economic development and renewal. The Area Director viewed it as a physically unattractive place for social workers, a factor which he felt contributed to their current understaffing and overload. The region was divided into four separate offices housing the social work teams. One office also contained a specialist advisory group - in effect a mini team designed to provide colleagues with working advice and resources on aspects of fostering, adoption, court and legal procedures, and facilities for the deaf. This team had its own leader, three senior social workers and three social workers. In addition to their advisory capacity, some members of the group carried their own case load.

Typically, the offices organised their work according to similar general principles. One or two social workers would undertake intake work. They would be responsible for handling all incoming

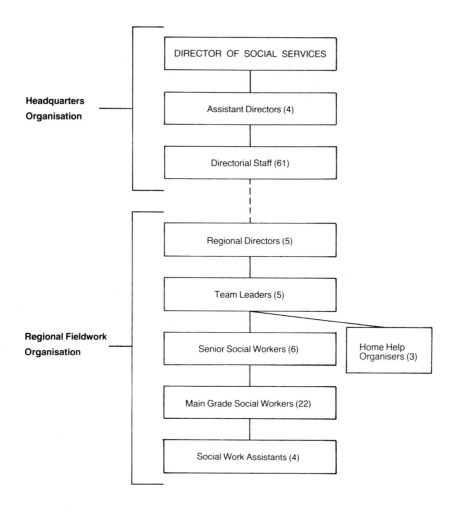

Figure 1.1 Social Services Department—Organisational Positions of Participants in the Study

client referrals or queries (after the reception-
ist), receiving personal visits, telephone calls and
letters, and deciding upon the next best course of
action. This might involve short-cycle or long-term
work for other members of their team, or a more
immediate 'solution' by the intake officer. Social
workers usually had preferences in their style of
work, some being generic - inclined to cover a broad
spectrum of activity - others possessing more specialist skills. These would apply to particular
problem areas, such as with young children, adolescents, the disabled, the elderly, the mentally handicapped, families, or the deaf.

The team leader and senior social workers were
responsible for supervising the work of the more
junior staff. All qualified social workers carried
a case load. The team leader would also have a
small number of clients, and would usually need to
be prepared to cover for absent or sick colleagues.
Social work assistants were not formally qualified
in social work, but were expected to 'assist' social
workers in tasks ranging from client visits to
aspects of administration. They were not normally
obliged to take on a case load themselves, nor
shoulder the statutory responsibilities of a qualified social worker. In practice, as we shall see,
things worked out rather differently. The teams
also employed organisers of a home help service, and
some had occupational therapists. All had clerical
support staff on the premises.

The area teams looked to headquarters for certain
aspects of policy and advice. This was a geographi-
cally remote, centralised organisation comprising a
director of social services, assistant directors of
various specialist concerns, and a wide range of
supportive staff.


THE PARTICIPANTS IN THE STUDY

All staff in the region, including clerical, were
offered the opportunity to participate in the study.
It soon transpired, however, that most interest was
amongst the social workers. Of a total group of 57,
40 people joined the project. In this final group
were all five team leaders, six senior social
workers, 22 'main grade' social workers, four social
work assistants and three home help organisers.

Their ages ranged from the early twenties to late fifties, the majority were female.


APPROACHES AND ACCESS

My first contact with the Social Services Department occurred in December 1977, but I did not start my actual research interviews until February 1980. The intervening 27 months represented a period of considerable delay, totally unforseeen events, and lengthy scene setting. A summary of the key features of this period helps to serve as an introduction to the research approach and to the organisation - its climate and main actors:

December 1977

The Director of Social Services is more than keen to do something to tackle stress issues which '...create big load problems for me and my staff, all the way down the line'. He describes a high incidence of symptoms associated with stress - withdrawal behaviour, absenteeism, migraines, and various psychosomatic complaints. He refers me to his Assistant Director of Fieldwork for further discussions. The Assistant Director reinforces her boss's concern, but also sees a stress study as likely to provide some political fodder for her, perhaps pointing to resources that she needs. But she encourages me to talk to some of her key headquarters staff first, as well as some staff in the regional offices.

January-May 1978

I have open-ended discussions on stress with a total of 16 people, including two area directors, two team leaders, two senior social workers, one main grade social worker and an area administrative officer. The discussions range across the major issues which each person felt was important in defining and accounting for stress - I do little to pre-channel their thoughts. A content analysis of their tape-recorded comments reveals three main themes:

1. All but two participants mention stress symptoms as part of their own work life, or as observed in colleagues. The psychological descriptions include irritability, anxiety, frustration and depression.

The more physical manifestations concern migraines, coronary diseases, fatigue, ulcers, arthritis and rheumatism. Gastric complaints are accepted philosophically as part and parcel of every day life in social work.

2.   A number of job-related concerns, such as the vulnerability felt by social workers when taking critical decisions on clients - particularly those involving babies; the feeling of overload; the lack of mutual support between colleagues; and the pressure of exceedingly long hours of work compounded by stand-by duties.

3.   The interface between area offices and headquarters.   Are the headquarter's staff advisers or directors?   Should they query local professional decisions?   A suspicion of headquarters requests, fuelled by doubts concerning the managerial capacity of social work professionals at headquarters.

July 1978

The initial findings are  included in a formal research proposal to the Director.   In this I suggest that the major research effort should focus initially on help for social workers in two regions.   I would offer myself as a counselling resource to those who wished to use me.   Essentially this would be a confidential service aimed at helping individual social workers develop relevant changes to alleviate their particular stress problems.   Our work together could involve other people - colleagues or managers,  who were part of the social worker's definition of the problem - although such action could require careful negotiation with the relevant parties.

There should be no feeling of obligation on social workers to participate, and the confidentiality of the events would be reinforced by the independent financing of my work.  I did not wish to be seen as responsible to any particular officer in the organisation as this could undermine the value of my independence - as would any 'final report' to the Director.   However, I would need to publish my findings for my research purposes, and this would be made clear to all those who wished to participate.

The area/headquarters difficulties would require separate attention. I proposed an initial series of small-group meetings of closely-linked headquarters and area staff. In these, the extent and dimensions of mutual differences could be explored, aided by methods such as role play and the re-enactment of events where 'communication' had failed. A second phase of group activity would be derived from the data collected from these meetings, leading to a commitment towards changes which could reduce points of stress.

August 1978

I learn that the Director had died after a serious illness.

September 1978

I discuss the proposal with the new Acting Director and the Assistant Director of Fieldwork. The Acting Director is reluctant to do anything that will 'rock the boat' during their period of uncertainty. He accepts, nevertheless, that the stress issues urgently require some action, and that my presence to date had raised the expectations that something would be done. He prefers a study of more limited scope, involving one major region and dropping the area/headquarters part. He is willing and eager to proceed as soon as I have obtained suitable funds.

July 1979

Twelve months of abortive fund-seeking have passed. The period is a considerably frustrating one for me. The principles and experience of this provide salutary example of the difficulties of funding non-traditional research (see Fineman, 1981). I plan somehow to manage on a shoe-string budget, and ask the Social Services Department to pay my travelling expenses. The Acting Director, who is now full Director, agrees to pay these costs. He still welcomes my work, particularly as '... there are the stresses of organisational changes in the wind'.

August 1979

I return to the Area Director to re-introduce the project and plan my introductions to his staff. He seems pleased to see me, but talks of a recent

internal research project which had 'gone dramati-
cally wrong' and which would increase scepticism
about new research ventures. However, he will support me. With some apprehension I agree to meet his
management team (five team leaders and an administration manager).

November 1979

The meeting with the management team. It begins
cautiously. I am told that many of the people who
had been involved in the previous internal research
were still smarting from its effects '...felt like
an interrogation...', '...abrogated the research
contract...', '...little trust...'. Yet no one
thinks I should not meet their social work team so
they can make up their own minds about the project.
There is the feeling that an outsider might build up
credibility and trust in a way which would be difficult for insiders. They are especially concerned
that I am not seen as a servant to headquarters, and
they are impressed by the individualistic and
flexible nature of the project.

December-January 1980

I meet each team separately to describe myself, my
interest in stress, and the nature of their possible
involvement with me. The climates vary from office
to office. Fairly cool, one-way giving of information in one; lively debate and much joking about
stress in another. One team interrogated me closely
about my own competence and for clarification (with
some incredulity) that here might be a project which
actually helps them. Shadows of previous research
lingered in their minds. I suggest that individuals
think about their desire to be involved and let me
know their decision when they feel ready.

February 1980

The first research meeting with an individual social
worker takes place.

   This saga indicates something of the method and
context of the research, but it also provides an
indication of the politics of an organisational
study, and the many hurdles that sometimes have to
be overcome. Any belief that organisations can be
simply 'set-up' for 'experimentation' in areas which

9

require the willing involvement of individuals on sensitive issues, is patently a questionable one. In many respects the researcher has to flow with the organisational tide, and acquire some appreciation of the history and culture of the setting he or she is entering. Indeed, as illustrated by the raised awareness of stress through my early interviews, the researcher becomes part of, and influences, that culture in some way, sometimes early on in the access process. It was not long before my presence was acknowledged in parts of the organisation I had not previously visited; there was talk of a stress project underway, and I was frequently labelled the 'stress man', a tag which I confess made me feel rather uncomfortable, but which seemed to provide others with a way of legitimising, and coping with, my activities.


BACKGROUND OF CHANGE

The project took place against a backcloth of organisational change. There were memories of previous changes, of intended (but aborted) changes, and expectations of future changes. Such a culture of change was reinforced by the intention of the new Director (previously acting Director) to remodel the whole service, and his plans were maturing during the period of the study. He envisaged a new grouping of client services, a reduction in the number of area offices, and the creation of new local and headquarter's management posts.

The aura of change permeated many people's views of their organisation: a few positively, some as a specific feature of their stresses, most as a long standing, generalised form of 'change shock'. As one newcomer noted:

> 'I've only recently joined this team and I've been arguing in our team meeting that we should help our clients manage the reorganisation because it would be their problem as well as ours. But the group just cut off from me - it was awful. As if they denied the issues. Eventually I got a response. They said they had been through possible reorganisations before, and they had rehearsed the feelings - they now cut off.

They didn't really _believe_ a reorganisation would come.'

The 'cutting off' that this man observed was a common reaction, or adaptation, to change:

'Most reorganisations have fallen apart. Great plans to start with, then they just evaporate: I just don't think about the next one!'

'So many changes have been planned, and nothing has happened. I just shut off - ignore it. I get on with my job.'

'This is the fifth reorganisation I've lived through. I think I'm reorganisation hardened to some extent. I've no special allegiance to this office, but for most people here it's a personal as well as professional injury that we should be carted off and centralised.'

'All the reorganisations that have failed! Reviews, re-integration of functions, centralisation, a new master plan. We get very cynical.'

Those who were unable to cope in this way were more specifically threatened by the change. They expressed fears about what lay ahead and the good things they might lose, especially supportive colleagues and comfortable working relationships. Some team leaders observed how the uncertainties of the new organisations had added that extra burden to some staff, increasing fractiousness and tears. Few social workers felt adequately consulted or involved in the process:

'Centralisation is being imposed on us by HQ. Local management has been told to shut up. Twice the Director has arranged to come here to talk to us, and both have been cancelled. It wouldn't be good social work to treat people that way. We are worried because we all think we've got something worth keeping now.'

'Uncertainties about what's going to happen are so high. The impression I get is a lot

of political deviousness from Director level,
which increases the anxiety for everyone.'

By the end of the project, a new organisational
structure had, in fact, materialised which also
involved a physical relocation. But behind all this
the social work continued, and quite 'normally' for
most.


TEAM CLIMATES

My work moved across five teams. Each had a distinct 'feel' to me, and some staff would make their
own observations - especially those who had worked
in, or travelled between, different teams. The
differences are important for appreciating some of
the findings to be reported in Parts II and III  of
the book, so I will attempt a brief description of
each.

Team A - 15 members, 11 participants

A tense, emotionally laden atmosphere. A feeling of
crisis, especially following a recent unfavourable
inspection from headquarters. The team leader was
often avoided by his staff and team meetings were
seen to be affairs fraught with anxiety. Team members talked of the high level of stress in the
majority of their colleagues.

Team B - 13 members, 10 participants

The least observed stress by members. An easy-going
feeling; a sense of order and space about events ...
'It's such a nice friendly atmosphere here; the team
leader is particularly interested in making team
meetings work and has time for you.'

Team C - 11 members, 8 participants

Fragmented - no overall cohesion. Some sub-groups
were mutually supportive and satisfied, others were
not. Stress was observed by members in approximately half of their colleagues. The team leader sensed
a disintegrating team, but saw too many organisational changes on the horizon, beyond his control,
to want to do anything to improve matters.

Team D - 7 members, 6 participants

The team leader appeared to go through the motions of managing his team, but he had withdrawn emotionally following acute work-stress of his own. Stress appeared particularly prevalent in this team, and people talked about 'only just about coping', with feelings of loneliness and lack of support.

Team E - 7 members, 5 participants

A very individualistic, professionally skilled team of people who were in advisory positions to other teams. Some forceful personalities. The team leader was connected to her members in a fairly loose, consultative role. Some used her, others did not. This left her with some unease as to her proper function. Members of this team were the first to make bids for my assistance in the project.

# 2 Intervention research and stress theory

The notion of researching a social or organisational phenomenon through the intervention and participative involvement of the researcher is one that has an auspicious but controversial history.  Traditional social scientists, of positivist inclination, argue that it is possible and necessary to separate the observer from the observed, a key to understanding the assumed laws of social conduct.  Such researches have tended to dominate social science in their quest for causal relationships, generally expressed through quantitative data.  At its extreme, scientific work of this ilk is viewed as quite distinct from the process of assisting in practical problems (Kerlinger, 1973).

But there is another view, reflecting a different root of knowledge, which suggests that it is naive to believe that investigators can somehow suspend their beliefs and preconceptions to access 'the truth'; they will be influencing their 'subjects' in a variety of ways (e.g. Argyris, 1980; Fineman and Mangham, 1983).  Thus, in certain respects, the investigator becomes part of the research data. Furthermore, if one is concerned with phenomena as experienced and 'naturally' expressed, rather than structured responses to tightly predetermined investigator constructs, then it is not too great a conceptual shift to believe that organisational behaviour is better understood through the investigator's involvement with organisational members, and the usefulness of such research is one measure of its validity. This type of collaborative researcher-organisation relationship is consistent with the views of writers such as Torbert (1976) and Herbst (1976), and can be seen in the work of 'action researchers', for example Lewin (1952), Sandford (1970) and Clark (1972).

Intervention research, as practised in this project, grew from this background. It was an approach that I had already developed to some degree for understanding the impact and stress of unemployment amongst middle class workers (Fineman, 1983). Its central feature is based on the proposition that the researcher's goals of understanding a participant's perceptions - beliefs, attitudes, feelings, concerns - vis-a-vis the researcher's theoretical interests, is best achieved through a collaborative, and facilitative, relationship. The research takes place with people rather than on them; it is based on a relationship where individuals can feel like participants in events where there is some genuine choice whether or not to take part, which have high credibility or face validity for them, and where they perceive a likelihood of some valued personal gain. The products of this relationship are data (usually qualitative) of high psychological validity; they tend to lack the gross filtering effect of 'researcher' and 'subject' posturing and instrumentation (but that does not mean they are not filtered or 'coloured'). Such validity is very different from the technical validity which can be demonstrated for traditional psychological studies; indeed, the 'rigour' attached to such works may succeed in obliterating much of the world as more freely constructed by the participant.

Unlike much action research, the end of intervention research as here conceived is not just client action or change; the researcher has his or her own particular conceptual interests. The intervention provides a vehicle for exploring these interests, perhaps describing a situation, generating new concepts, or testing hunches or hypotheses. This is the quid pro quo of the research. It is an open declaration that the researcher has an agenda of his or her own which will interweave with the very

substance of the interventions. For the participant, the researcher's concerns should appear in a
relatively non-intrusive, low profile form, effectively indistinguishable from the intervention
process. The researcher, though, has an eye firmly
on certain theoretical/conceptual concerns which
form the basis of his or her academic pursuits - in
the present case, stress.


## STRESS

In thinking about stress I was guided by a framework
I had found helpful on previous occasions (interested readers can find a detailed exposition in
Fineman, 1979). Its essence, as employed in this
study, defines stress as a psychological state of
high-anxiety, reflected in self-descriptions such as
being 'very unhappy', 'fearful', 'overwhelmed', and
'all screwed-up inside'. Such states may be accom-
panied by physical symptoms; gastric upsets, headaches, migraines and back pains being amongst the
milder. Gastric ulcers, high blood pressure and
heart disease are some of the more serious
illnesses.

Stress is seen to follow an individual's inability
to cope with threatening problems or difficulties.
'Threat' is pivotal here. Feelings of threat emerge
when a sensitive or vulnerable aspect of oneself is
perceived to be under attack in some way. What is
threatening to one person may, of course, not be so
for another - depending upon personality differences, such as self esteem, particular fears or
susceptibility to anxiety, and also the social context of the event. For example, an inexperienced
social worker may feel exceedingly threatened by how
her competence is judged when she represents a
client in a court of law, while an experienced
senior worker is not too bothered by such views.
Some social workers may desperately require affirmation of the worth of their efforts, so they are
particularly sensitive to criticism from clients or
colleagues. Others, though, may be inured to such
criticism, relying on well-tested personal
standards.

Feeling threatened is an uncomfortable state of
affairs, characterised by rising anxiety - but it is
not stress. Stress, as conceptualised here, results

from failing to remove the threat; a compounding of the anxiety from the threat with that from failure to cope. 'Removing' threat can occur in a number of different ways. One can fend off the threat by not recognising its existence, or by avoiding contact with it (often an unconscious process). A social worker may stop thinking about certain very difficult clients, or may find plausible reasons for not visiting them. Such reactions help to reduce the alarm and fear of threat by blocking tension build-up, but they are, by their very nature, reactive rather than proactive; they deal more with the emotional reactions to a problem. In addition, maintaining effective defence is costly on energy; it can soon deplete available resources, leaving the individual exhausted and vulnerable.

Threat may be tackled 'head on', a perhaps painful confrontation with the difficulty or problem. New, low-threat ways of seeing things may emerge from this process, or different forms of managing; the threat has been dealt with 'at source' and stress avoided. Yet such actions may fail. No easy solution is found and each new confrontation ends up reinforcing the previous failure. A cycle of increasing stress results, and whatever defences are left need to be mustered to offer some form of protection.

At this point, stress may be unavoidable - it is an unpleasant fact of life, in the short term at least. Under such circumstances, palliative actions may be all that is left - ways of managing tension, keeping anxiety at bearable levels and protecting oneself from the ravages of the most damaging features of stress. Attempts in this direction might also help to facilitate future confrontations. However, all this is much easier said than done. Typically, people who are highly stressed feel too stressed to do much to help themselves - a depressing state of affairs for them, and others.

Stress, in these terms, is a 'bad' thing, psychologically and perhaps physically debilitating and as such the less of it the better. This is certainly not to suggest that some tension in life is unproductive. Much research, and common wisdom, points to the need for certain levels of tension to help us to perform activities. The optimum points will vary considerably between people and between activities,

17

but the tension level associated with stress is seen as considerably beyond this point of facilitation.

## The framework in practice

These notions of stress were used as an orienting set of concepts within the counselling format described in the next section. The principles were discussed openly with social workers, and they guided the emphasis and exploration of the counselling: they therefore affected some of the content and shape of the research data. In summary, the framework can be seen to highlight the following four areas:

-   Signs of stress, e.g. illness, psychological difficulties, changes in behaviour
-   Sources of threat, e.g. other people, crisis clients, failure situations, non-work demands, particular work tasks or settings
-   Personal vulnerabilities, e.g. fears, ambitions, security, affection, self esteem, sense of purpose, competence
-   Coping, e.g. effective and ineffective defences, confronting threats, anxiety management

Help at managing stress focusses on identifying sources of threat and, within the context of an individual's personality make-up and personal vulnerabilities, assisting that person to cope more effectively. This may involve help towards constructing different ways of confronting a difficulty, or building more adequate defences - learning to live with a seemingly insoluble problem. The way these principles were operationalised should become clearer in the next section, and in Part III.


## A HELPING RATIONALE

The aim of the helping, or interventionist, activity was to assist social workers with their stress problems, as well as to generate research data on social worker stress. I used counselling to enable social workers to explore their stress difficulties, achieve new understandings and act in ways to reduce their stress.

I have been impressed by Egan's (1975) argument that effective counselling can be viewed, in large measure, as a social influence process. The counsellor helps the client towards new coping strategies and skills for living by the direct influence of care, understanding and collaboration. In achieving these ends, helping can be 'integratively eclectic' (Brammer and Shostrom, 1968), drawing upon a range of theories on individual and social conduct. My own position reflects writings on behaviour in organisations and organisational change and development (e.g. Huse, 1980; French and Bell, 1973; Schein, 1969; Weick, 1979). There has been no concerted approach to stress in this literature (Golembiewski, 1982), but certain of its tenets and techniques contribute in that direction. For example, there is much concern for individual well-being and the dilemmas posed by the effects of organisational procedures on individual expression. The importance of viewing change and adaptation 'phenomenologically', through the eyes of the actor (e.g. Douglas, 1970; Weick, 1979; Goodman and Kurke, 1982), focusses our attention on individually construed meanings in the helping process: discovering the nature of the client's personal realities to generate the essential raw material for helper and client to work upon. At this level the helper assists change by aiding others to clarify their thoughts and articulate their ideas. Clients receive the attention of a 'conceptual therapist' (Weick, 1982) who helps them to generate their own solutions to their problems - a likely more rewarding and enduring process than accepting 'expertly' imposed solutions.

In placing the social worker firmly at the centre of the stage, as a self-responsible individual, I am not denying that that person will be part of a complex and interrelated network of structures and relationships - his or her own family and non-work life, clients, offices, a variety of departments and agencies within and outside social services, a local authority, and a country with certain government policies on social welfare. It is likely that some of these will powerfully influence work perceptions and the quality of working life. To reject this would leave us 'blaming the victim' for his or her predicament, whatever, and ignoring many sociological and social psychological bases of human behaviour. But a phenomenological view of behaviour and change asserts that there is no necessary correlation between altering 'out there' conditions, such as structures and policies, and a particular individual's attitude or behaviour change. The filter of personal prejudices, expectations, fears and needs provides each person with a unique blend of realities. Moreover, the 'loose coupling' of levels and departments in a social service organisation creates many halting points, twists and turns, to ensure that structural changes emerging from one level (usually the top) are unlikely to be reflected or emulated across levels. Individual responses will be shaped more by local conditions - mutual ties, beliefs, norms and expectations. It is here that stress and change are effected.

Yet, as far as stress is concerned, I am suspicious of the idealism of some writers in the 'humanistic', 'self-actualisation' vein of organisational thinking: that somehow organisational life can be re-formulated to be stress and strife free, collaborative and self actualising. As some observers have indicated, political intrigue, competitive battles, mutual suspicion and power games have been a curiously enduring feature of organisational life. They form the excitement and rewards for some, and the 'cut-throat' ethic, in various guises, is accorded a high social value in our political and economic culture (Pettigrew, 1972; Pfeffer, 1981). Moreover there are powerful people, 'reality definers', who would be hard to influence by some, and impossible by others (Mangham, 1979). Consequently I see interventions in stress needing to steer through such realities. Help is geared towards action that is feasible, within the client's area of control, and time is spent in working towards discovering manageable 'bits' of the problem. Indeed the web of political influences inside an organisation can markedly affect the complexion of where one can work; so energy is best placed where political sympathy lies. This way of thinking reminds us that sometimes certain sources of stress will be inaccessible to modification (e.g. Pines et al, 1981), so concentrating on ways of living with them may be a more productive direction of effort.

Counselling phases

Egan (1975) views counselling in terms of a series of progressive stages directed towards the client's action, each stage demanding particular counsellor skills and behaviour. I have adapted Egan's notions in Figure 2.1 to illustrate the structure of my own counselling, some of the typical counsellor-behaviours, and the link between the counselling and the research data. The four phases accurately represent the range of my activity, but should not be seen as a literal representation of what happened. Not always was the order of events neat and sequential, and the time scale varied considerably. All of the phases were collapsed into a single two-hour meeting for each of 20 social workers. Nine others had two meetings, two met with me three times, two four times, and five had five meetings. The longest series was six meetings with one person.

Part III of this book is devoted to an examination of the key processes within Phases II, III and IV. It gives an indication of what I actually did, and how social workers responded. The following discussion outlines the aims and structure of each of the phases.

Phase I - <u>Introduction</u> and <u>orientation</u>   A social worker's willingness to meet me in a counselling relationship very much depended on my credibility in their eyes. Who was I? What did I want? Who was I working for? Could I be trusted? What was in it for them? These were amongst the direct and implied questions that I received during my introductory meeting with groups of social workers and (separately) with their managers. In social influence terms, I needed to be perceived as sufficiently expert, trustworthy and attractive for social workers to enter a relationship where they would be, to some extent, subject to my social control. I recognised that this early stage in relationship building was a critical one for the viability and success of my activities. It was complicated by the coolness and impersonal atmosphere I encountered in addressing some large team meetings, a more difficult setting for communication than the less formal groups. Additionally, as mentioned earlier, the legacy of 'bad research' had generally soured the air, and this became an issue for me to act against - an uncomfortable position as some of that work had been conducted by existing internal researchers.

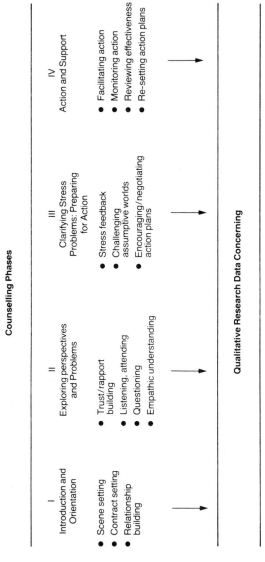

**Counselling Phases**

| I<br>Introduction and Orientation | II<br>Exploring perspectives and Problems | III<br>Clarifying Stress Problems: Preparing for Action | IV<br>Action and Support |
|---|---|---|---|
| ● Scene setting<br>● Contract setting<br>● Relationship building | ● Trust/rapport building<br>● Listening, attending<br>● Questioning<br>● Empathic understanding | ● Stress feedback<br>● Challenging assumptive worlds<br>● Encouraging/negotiating action plans | ● Facilitating action<br>● Monitoring action<br>● Reviewing effectiveness<br>● Re-setting action plans |

**Qualitative Research Data Concerning**

— The meaning and experience of stress: stress signs, threats, coping
— The social worker's self and personality: fears, vulnerabilities
— The social worker's experience of work: specific problems, crises
— How change can and cannot be achieved: attempted action, experienced change

Figure 2.1  Counselling Phases and Research Data

In the meetings I emphasised my independence in the organisation, outlined my own ideas on stress, and gave a glimpse of the counselling/research process that could lie ahead. I also described some of my previous work and pointed out that it was their own individual stress issues which were the subject of interest and help. I described myself as a resource for those who wished to use me - but one that they should contemplate awhile before contacting me or their team leader, should they be interested. I was keen that meetings should not be left with the impression of a hidden agenda which would contradict the ethos of the research and aggravate the existing alienation towards 'being studied'. Articulating my models of intervention was a step in this direction (they were frameworks for their use as well as mine), as was my attempt to be clear about my own research interests and their part in them.

Phase II - Exploring perspectives and problems This phase involved individual meetings with those who had decided to take part in the study. My purpose was to cultivate the seeds of rapport more intensely and personally and to respond to the social worker with (in Egan's words) 'respect and empathy'. It was my opportunity to see how the social worker defined and shaped his or her world, and the assumptions that were displayed. I would do this through attending, listening and empathic feedback - verbally and non-verbally. I began to sense some of the world that they were sensing, and started to help them to explore themselves and their experiences. Although this process was triggered by my question, 'What, if anything, does stress mean to you in your work?', I would deliberately encourage them to talk around their stress areas and settle at those points which concerned them most. I would prompt them to expand or illustrate issues through specific instances and concrete examples, especially on the nature and substance of perceived problems and other aspects of the stress framework - signs of stress, sources of threat, personal vulnerabilities and coping styles.

Discussions were tape recorded, with their permission. Only one person, who was very distressed when I saw her, was uneasy about this - so I made notes after the session instead. All of our meetings were in private rooms, of varying degrees of comfort. I

was sometimes able to rearrange the furniture in a
manner which I felt would be more relaxing for us.

Some would begin hesitantly, unsure of their
proper role and a little anxious about the process.
I would talk about this as much as necessary to
allay their uncertainties and concerns.  Most
people, however, soon relaxed into what appeared
natural but intensive self declaration.  As social
workers they were an articulate group, many of them
cognisant of the language and concepts of stress.
But talking in these terms about themselves, to an
outsider, was a rare and often unique event.

Phase III - Clarifying stress problems:  Preparing
for action  This phase would normally merge with the
previous one.  My purpose was to focus the social
worker's explorations onto specific, actionable,
stress problems.  I would begin to integrate and
summarise the overt and covert data - what Egan
refers to as 'advanced accurate empathy'.  In practice this meant feeding back to the social worker
specific parts of what he or she had said or
implied, but re-set within the stress framework.
This was usually a gradual and iterative process in
which I would attempt to get as close as possible to
the most painful, threatening problems - where it
was likely that the social worker's motivation to
change would be greatest.  How close to the 'mark' I
was getting was normally indicated by the extent of
the social worker's affirmation or ownership of my
statements - indicated by puzzled looks and corrections to my interpretations (off the mark), to
winces, grimaces or cries such as 'That's exactly
it!' (closer to the mark).  This process was sometimes a difficult and testing one.  My feedback
could challenge defensive, protective, smokescreens.
How directly confronting I could be depended upon
how vulnerable I felt the social worker to be.  It
could be a delicate process for us both as I
adjusted the pace of our discussions and feedback,
engaged in personal self-disclosure, and commented
on my here-and-now impressions of what was happening.  All the time I had in mind the next best
direction or behaviour which would help the social
worker define and accept his or her difficulties
more easily and more clearly.

Sometimes the effects of this were sudden and
cathartic - such as when social workers talked

enthusiastically about 'things coming together'. The counselling, it would seem, had provided new understandings, new insights and a new angle from which to view problems. Relevant action plans would follow, unprompted - 'I know what I must do next - have it out directly with my team leader', 'It's now obvious that I have to seek support outside of this office', 'Why on earth I keep taking on that type of work without complaining, I just don't know. It will change from tomorrow!'. New understandings could profoundly influence attitudes - a persistent threat now seemed innocuous and irrelevant. 'Action', in such cases, was intrapsychic - a reconceptualisation had removed the threat, for the time being at least.

The simplicity, or complexity, of change was partly a matter of the type of problems that the social worker presented. For some it was a readily identified current crisis which could be focussed on a particular work difficulty or procedure. For others, there were overlaps between a number of stress-connected problems inside and outside of work. And still others chose to 'talk through' past struggles and crises, things which now affected their attitudes towards the job, and style of coping. Not surprisingly a fairly clear-cut solution to a problem was easier to locate when that problem was relatively self-contained and immediate.

Spontaneous solutions, though, did not always arise. There were individuals who clearly wanted to do something, but did not know what. I regarded directive help from myself as crucial at this stage. I share a view, expressed by a number of writers on counselling and personal change, that for some people raised awareness is an important precursor to change, but without the necessary follow-up skills and support, knowing the 'shape of the beast' alone can serve to increase anxiety and helplessness. So assistance can be required in ways of re-thinking problems and threat - presenting alternative frames of reference which might reduce the onerousness of a task, a relationship, or whatever. I found such interventions most successful when they reflected fairly peripheral perceptions of self or others; perceptions based upon taken-for-granted expectations which had rarely, if ever, been challenged. I could sometimes contest the social workers' assumptions, personal definitions, or even reverse their customary logic, and then examine with them the consequences of the new belief on their problems. This tack was least productive when a social worker's way of thinking on a problem reflected very 'deep' fears or anxieties. It is arguable whether more intensive psychodynamic intervention, or other forms of personality therapy, should be the appropriate response at this point. I was not qualified to offer such assistance, nor was the counselling setting suited to it. I could, however, suggest ways in which stress and tension might be better controlled given the difficulty in tackling underlying 'causes' to the problem. Such advice included various methods of physical relaxation and ways of escaping anxiety and developing support - all proffered and discussed in a practicable form, geared to the particular individual.

Some action plans involved the social worker's commitment to a specific new behaviour or behaviours. I would suggest ideas for the social worker to consider, reformulate, accept or reject - such as: 'What do you think would happen if you took that problem straight to your supervisor?', 'How might Bill respond if you invited him to talk things over, with me present?', 'Do you think you could diary, right now, a day a week to handle all that paperwork that you find so formidable?', 'What if you experimented with speaking up at team meetings? What do you think would happen?'. I encouraged and supported - emotionally and, if necessary, practically - any suitable action the social worker was willing to take. I capitalised on the 'helping power' that I had acquired to act as a rewarder of effort: they would receive my concern and attention on an important aspect of their lives if they carried out their action plans. Sometimes I spelled out my support in negotiative terms: 'If you try that I will make sure I help you work through your experiences and help you figure out where you've got to. If things don't work out, we will try and discover why.' I assumed that success would bring its own rewards, reducing or eliminating my role as an 'external reinforcer'.

Phase IV - Action and support  The final counselling phase was for those social workers who 'went away and did something' - either in re-thinking the nature of their problems, or in trying new behaviours. I would help them to evaluate their

26

progress and encourage new directions of thought if necessary - an activity that sometimes took place a number of times as new actions, and sometimes new problems, evolved. When someone had not proceeded as planned, I would help them look at the reasons why - as often the anticipated action turned out to be too threatening to undertake, or inappropriately linked to the problem. At this point we would look for new ways forward.

Reports of something 'working', a plan 'paying off', were usually happy if not euphoric occasions. I would share their obvious joy and stress release - more so in that I often felt that some of their risks in 'stepping out' were also my risks, given my close involvement with them. But the dominant, more sober, activity which concerned me was to help the social worker extract maximum learnings from what had gone on, hopefully to provide some future protection against stress.

My personal resources - time, energy and coping capacities - did not extend beyond this natural completion of the counselling phases. I parted from the social worker when there was an overt or tacit agreement that 'things had been worked through for the present'.

Counsellor support

I found the pressures of working on this project sometimes intense. It required the management of interpersonally demanding situations, together with the need for some personal space to reflect on the content of research meetings and plan details of feedback. Unlike traditional 'distanced' research, it was not possible, nor desirable, to plan all moves. Some agility was required in improvising responses according to the varying interpretations and meanings attached to interactions as they occurred (Mangham, 1982). Furthermore, my activities were based very much on me, and the relationships I had cultivated; I could not simply call in another researcher or assistant to help me out.

Ironically, I discovered that I was living through some of the client-type issues that the social workers themselves confronted in their own work (see Part II) - such as liking and disliking certain clients, feeling taken for granted, getting over-involved with some people, feeling impotent in face of chronic client stresses, and trying to manage the effect of client issues in my private life. I recognised, early on in my work, that I needed my own particular support so that I could talk through what I was doing, and avoid debilitating stress in myself. A colleague at work provided this for me - an invaluable aid during the early months of the research. He would reflect back to me my worries and plans and help me to re-think the directions in which I was going.

I would find myself talking about my concerns more vicariously - especially with interested colleagues and my wife. Also it was therapeutic (as well as a valuable research record) to talk into my tape recorder while driving home from a counselling session. To this anonymous machine I would spill out my immediate impressions and anxieties, and set up ideas and questions for later consideration.

Towards the end of the research I noticed, almost incidentally, that I was using external support less and less. The drama of the emotional load was still there, but I had learned to cope by better under-standing the range of demands placed upon me. I had found ways of 'switching off' or compartmentalising the multitude of others' problems that I was hearing and sharing. The early threats of 'doing things right', appearing competent and managing the quality and quantity of the load, felt much reduced. I had now some practised routines which felt comfortable - I was generally in control of myself and my work.


THE RESEARCH ANALYSIS

The research aimed to uncover and explore some of the features and dynamics of social worker stress. Data from all the aforementioned work were used to this end. I reanalysed the tape recordings follow-ing principles of qualitative analysis (Bogdan and Taylor, 1975; Lofland, 1976). Initially, categories of stress experience, concern, threat, problems, difficulties and coping were recorded for each person. I then sorted these written statements into the 'sense-making' pictures which are presented in the next part of the book. This brief outline makes light of an exceedingly laborious process of analysis; yet it is one that intimately engages the researcher in the patterning and shaping of what initially seems a disconnected mass of comments.

In Part III I call upon an extra source of data - the social workers' retrospections of their experiences in the research. Eight weeks after our final meeting, I sent each social worker a letter asking them to describe their current views on our work together, and any changes they perceived in themselves and in others which they believed could be attributed to the counselling.

# Part II
# The pattern of findings

# 3 A framework

A content-analysis of participants' perceptions generated some 90 categories of experience - a broad range of views about self, others, the job, the organisation and the profession. A close look at these, with notions of stress firmly in mind, produced the more parsimonious picture presented in Figure 3.1.

There are four major facets of a social worker's life which interact and influence stress reactions. These are: characteristics of the self - personality qualities and coping skills; perceived job features, ranging from office politics to client pressures; home pressures - such as demands of a marriage, managing a household and children; and the quantity and quality of personal support within the job, and outside of work.

This highly simplified representation disguises the complexity of interactions. For example, a social worker's self image or predisposition to anxiety would likely affect how certain job features are perceived; a self-reliant individual is probably less critical of organisational support. Being highly stressed will itself 'colour' certain perceptions - such as of self worth, 'demanding' clients, and home tensions. Yet this broad classification

provides some guides and signposts within an otherwise bewildering array of perceptions.  Let me now
fill-out the framework with the expressions of the
social workers themselves.

Figure 3.1:  Facets of Social Worker Stress

# 4  Stress responses

Few social workers had difficulty in articulating
the nature and significance of their stress experiences.  In a sense they were a stress-sophisti-
cated group where the language of stress was part of
their professional vocabulary.  Each revealed
personal reactions - feelings, behaviours, physical
changes - which characterised their specific stress
responses.  My interest was in expressions of
episodic or chronic stress, current or recent, which
were qualitatively distinct from the everyday
'niggles' or more ephemeral irritants of work life.
Such a discrimination was marked by the depth and
sharpness of the reactions described, and also by
the context of threat and failure to cope.  (See
Parts I and III for details of how I focussed on
such data.)

For some, a whole mix of psychological, behavioural and physical reactions epitomised their stress:

'I start running round in circles getting
more and more frustrated, feeling I've got a
long list of things to do and I've spent
three days doing just the first one!  I wind
up chewing my finger nails out, or smoking
very heavily, kicking the door. Frustration,
anxiety. It's "what's happening?"  There

aren't enough hours in the day. I feel physically drained and shattered. Some people in the team almost go under with this syndrome - but never quite go under.'

'Anger is not usual for me, so it's a sign of stress. Because of the tremendous tension this job creates at home I find I can't concentrate; migraines. I feel apathetic, lethargic, or just tired and screwed up physically inside. This has just come to a head in the last few weeks.'

Physical reactions dominated some people's descriptions - such as muscle tension, asthma, exhaustion, migraines, infections, headaches, colds, backaches, and gastric upsets. Indeed, being physically sick emerged as an acceptable norm of behaviour amongst the social workers, providing an organisationally legitimate reason to take time off to 'recharge' or escape stress. Stress illness was talked about in matter-of-fact terms, rather than self-pityingly. Most staff were concerned about the organisational consequences of absenteeism, however few did not see the 'need' for it, and the safety valve that it provided. In the words of one social worker:

'It may sound surprising, but it is really an accepted part of social work to go sick. In social work your colleagues accept, at an unconscious level, your need to be ill.'

'Being ill' was graphically described by some:

'When one or two crises blow, that's OK. But when you get three or four, it's too much. I tear about, don't eat properly - you can't eat regularly in this job anyway. So at the end of such a bout, it affects me physically; I get run down and tired, I had a patch two weeks ago - taken me two to three weeks to pull out of it.'

'Stress - oh yes. I was off because I put my neck out and I get migraines. Also eye infections. I've just had to deal with a battered baby and a child who absconded - that's what it does to me.'

'I get skin problems when I'm under stress.
Such as when I recently received a hand-
written memo from the Area Director repriman-
ding me for not attending a meeting.  But I
was so overloaded with casework!'

'Last year I didn't think I suffered from
stress at all - then I got physical symptoms.
Chest pains, breathlessness, yet the doctor
said nothing was physically wrong.  Things
irritate me so much here they actually make
me ill.'

'I take flight into stress.  I've had appal-
ling problems organising my team.  This has
led to back problems, time off work, depression, anxiety, and other illnesses associated
with stress.'

'Physically I get exhausted.  This year I've
had more days off than ever before.  Colds,
arthritis.  My clients just aren't getting a
fair deal.'

'I seem to have biological warning systems.
I have just gone through a very heavy situation here and my skin gets covered with a
rash.'

Approximately half of the social workers talked of
specific psychological signs of stress, such as
chronic tension, anxiety, panic, feeling overwhelmed, frustration and inability to relax:

'I get so panicky.  Last week I had to cope
with a case in court which I was dreading; a
kid who needed a residential place, but HQ
wouldn't give me one.  I was a quivering mass
- I had to take the oath and confirm.'

'Struggling with some clients is utterly
draining - leaves me feeling dead; tired and
depressed.'

'I see myself in a stressful job.  I see
stress in others.  There are times when I can
say I feel under a lot of stress, yet I don't
perceive how I'm operating differently.  I
feel frustrated, angry, impatient - coupled
with feelings of immobilisation.  There's an

awful lot that needs doing at once, so I feel stressed.'

'As I drive to work in the morning, my anxiety level gets higher and higher. By the end of the day, I can't cope any more - get irritable and headachey.'

'It's the little things that get to me, those odd remarks from colleagues. I get a sick feeling, wanting to get out, fed up. It builds up with me.'

'Lots of weird things happen to me, especially since recently I've been judged as "unsatisfactory" in my work. I get aggressive, tense, and abrupt. After work I feel quite shattered.'

Some of this group also highlighted certain changes in their behaviour when stressed. Although not necessarily an exclusive reaction, they found themselves doing things differently, oddly:

'One expression of my stress is having unrealistic expectations of other people. They "ought" to know this or that. A displacement of my not coping.'

'I do recognise stress in myself. It's not the obvious signs like bad temper - I smoke more, and get really fatigued if things are particularly bad.'

'When that last crisis hit me I couldn't eat for days. It has caused me so much stress. It's coloured everything I'm doing; I'm questioning everything.'

'I smoke more. Get emotional when talking about a particular kid because it means a lot to me. I get really angry with my team leader.'

'I wake up at night thinking about work. I get run down, depressed, and become ill. Typically, over a holiday or long weekend I develop a cold.'

'My performance drops and I get headaches - that's my stress. I tend to move bits of paper around but don't achieve very much. We're in the people business; when something goes wrong, people get hurt.'

## THE RANGE OF STRESS RESPONSES

The foregoing accounts portray psychological, behavioural and physical signs of stress, not unlike those typically reported in the general research literature on stress. Some social workers were more 'physical' in their reactions than others, although overall, the range of responses was exceedingly broad. These are summarised, for the total group, in Table 4.1.

## BURNOUT

Research, particularly in America, has focussed on one particular response to overwhelming stress amongst those in the helping professions - burnout (e.g. Cherniss, 1980; Pines et al, 1981). There is some debate about the precise nature of burnout, although a recent synthesis by Maslach (1982) gives us a guide. It appears to represent (a) a state of emotional and physical exhaustion with a lack of concern for the job, and a low trust of others, (b) a depersonalisation of clients; a loss of caring and cynicism towards them, and (c) self-deprecation and low morale, and a deep sense of failure. The seeds of burnout are said to be sown early in career through unrealistically high expectations of what can be achieved (Edelwich and Brodsky, 1980). Unchecked this can begin a steady process of disillusionment and apathy. Those who care for others may be most vulnerable to burnout because of the heightened emotional demands of the job, coupled with the desire to see client change in difficult circumstances. It is a dramatic, protective disengagement following a failure to cope in other ways.

I detected four social workers who seemed to be in, or near burnout. It is quite possible that those experiencing burnout were the least likely to join the project because of the feelings of chronic hopelessness that can accompany the condition.

| PSYCHOLOGICAL | BEHAVIOURAL | PHYSICAL |
|---|---|---|
| Tense, worried, anxious | Constantly questioning own actions | High blood pressure |
| Anxiety-depression | Not eating | Heart racing |
| Screwed up inside | Taking tranquillisers | Skin disease |
| Tied-up in knots | Insomnia | Backache |
| Panicky | Freezing | Coughs and colds |
| Tearful | Distancing | Arthritis |
| Pressured | Unrealistic expectations of others | Breathlessness |
| Stewing over difficulties | Running round in circles | Muscle tension |
| Woozy feeling | Reacting too quickly | Headaches |
| Unable to relax | Switching off/escaping | Migraine |
| Frustrated | Putting up barriers | Eye infections |
| Overwhelmed | Jumping from problem to problem | Asthma |
| Loss of confidence | Underperforming | Nausea |
| Self doubt | Short tempered/ impatient | Gastric upsets |
| | Too aggressive | Fatigue/exhaustion |
| | Too impatient | |

Table 4.1: SIGNS AND SYMPTOMS OF STRESS

The most extreme example was Jim, a young social worker whose disillusionment permeated his job experience:

'When I first qualified, I was keen, eager and excited. I wasn't here for two weeks when my supervisor said "You're wearing the ticket - everyone's the same when they come out of college. Nothing's different. Calm down and you'll soon learn." That smashed me - like a whack across my face. I always thought social workers were nice people - keen to help you. Actually, if I was a client I would think that there are only five social workers here that I could trust and do their job well. This really frightens me. I'm tired generally. I want the job but the responsibility at times is too much, with all the other things going on. My body is giving me warning signs. It's like having a clogged artery. I feel like chopping it off and hoping a new one will grow. There's nothing holding me here.'

Another worker, Ann, had been recently bereaved, which triggered thoughts and feelings about her emotional competence for the job:

'For the last six to eight months, I've been asking myself whether I should continue in social work - whether I've got enough to give - and I've run out. The job can be so depressing. Most of the people we deal with are the inadequates. They're not going to change. You can't make up for years of deprivation. It makes you wonder - why do we bother? Why do we put up with the hassle? I really don't know. It's ridiculous when you look at the time and energy you put into someone when you know there will probably be no returns. And a lot of pain you get sometimes. Like a kid of mine just come up to court again. I could kill him - stupid idiot. It means that everything I've done for two years is wasted. He'll probably go to Borstal.'

Martin was not as extreme in his reaction as Ann, but seemed to be moving towards disengagement from the job, typical of burnout:

'There's a difficulty in overcoming the feeling that one is indispensable. Although I did it yesterday - I just didn't turn up to appointments. Do I always have to be beholden to my clients - explain myself to them? I don't know how I'm going to find the energy to cope; that's beginning to be a worry. One way of dealing with it is to begin to cut off from people. Be non-caring to clients and colleagues.'

The last example concerns a senior social worker who had recently become part of a new advisory team. Much to her consternation she found little authority or challenge in the post:

'I feel a general low in motivation, even to change the circumstances at work. Life crisis - wasted education? The job asks more of me than I can give - I have to "act" rather than "react". Do I justify my salary? I am so bored.'

She was chronically underloaded in her job and felt like a fish out of water. She could find no ways of facing this, so she backed off, feeling depressed and a failure.


FEELING GOOD?

The responses so far reported give the strong impression that a social worker's life is simply not a happy one. Given that stress reactions were of prime interest in the study these were the ones that were, naturally, most discussed and catalogued. But it would be a misrepresentation to take this picture as a complete one. For many participants, stress issues were phasic or episodic. Between such periods, a whole range of emotions were experienced. While the glow from success was generally an elusive experience (a theme to be expanded in the next chapter), some social workers were able to pinpoint those circumstances when they felt good, deeply satisfied - perhaps joyful.

Working with the elderly was one such situation:

'I don't want gratitude but I want to see someone's pleased with your efforts. And you

get this from the elderly. They ask for so
little, really. Like getting an old lady
into a day centre which opens up her life,
giving her new friends. She claims it's the
best thing that ever happened to her. You
<u>feel</u> you've done something. You generally
<u>work</u> hard for this in social work.'

'It's the elderly and the handicapped who
seem more grateful and rewarding than the
younger generation. They do seem to be more
pleased when I've visited them, and problems
don't often reappear. They say to me "that
<u>did</u> help me when you talked to me".'

'A client can say "thank you" and that's
lovely. The best thing said to me by a
client was calling me the best listener she
had ever known. I don't think I am, so that
was lovely! Families thank you, but better
still, you can <u>see</u> more improvement in an old
person - eating better, better health, less
confused.'

By way of contrast, certain satisfactions were
derived from exercising administrative and political
skills:

'Sometimes the rewards and success of the job
is actually finding a place in a children's
home, or getting a seventeen year old off a
Detention Centre. Last week I got a success
in court by persuading them to put a kid on
community service rather than into a Detention Centre. I was happy about that.'

'Real joy for me is finding a placement for a
kid having spent all day knocking on doors
for him!'

And for a team leader...

'For me, going to management meetings is
exhilarating - especially the back-stage
wheeling and dealing. This is the part of
the job I like the most! I'd hate to go back
knocking on doors and seeing individual
clients again.'

Rewards came from working in people's lives with some indication, albeit sometimes slight, that they were moving in a 'better' direction:

'People matter. In most cases, you can see some small positive change, and that's something for me. If you can see a kid who's got settled in a foster home after three years of chuntering around the place. Or if you see they can just say something to somebody that they couldn't say before, or they can admit one little bit of what is one of their problems. In most cases you can see something of that, even those going fast downhill - some self-awareness.'

'Well, ironically it is satisfying to point out to people that they don't need the resources of the Department - help them to see things in another perspective. Also getting a decision accepted by the team that a person does not need long-term help. To be somehow instrumental in helping people solve their problems is satisfying.'

'I'm fascinated about other people's lives. I enjoy the challenge in meeting people's problems - fitting the answers to the problems. Getting people to relate to me is exceedingly rewarding.'

Getting results, for some, was tied in with the length of intervention. There were those who saw long-term and family work as most rewarding, whilst others lauded the benefits of short-term work. The 'short-termers' were the most vociferous:

'I handle all the short-term work on intake. It's so exciting not to know what will be present tomorrow! It's so much less stressful than long-term work as it doesn't go on for ever.'

'I prefer short-term work than long-term work. More satisfaction and scope. You can see more things through from beginning to end. See the problem, deal with it, finish it. I like that - personally satisfying.'

# 5 Job features

There was a group-pattern of job influences which contributed to stress, despite marked individual variations. Most frequently mentioned (some 80 per cent of participants) were the local, immediate, inside-office experiences. These were seen as some of the major realities of 'being' a social worker - the nitty-gritty, political thrust of social work life. Participants spoke of the nature of their load, the crises in their work, supervisory relationships and working in inappropriate specialisms. Social work assistants drew attention to the ambiguities of their role.

The second most influential force were the clients. Sixty per cent of the group gave graphic accounts of the emotional peculiarities and costs of working with people, especially children, whose welfare, and sometimes lives, depended upon the wisdom of their intervention.

Three other areas were identified, each by approximately one third of the group. The first concerned the elusiveness of success in social work - the rarity of seeing positive results for one's efforts, or even not knowing what such results should look like. The second focussed on vibrations from the broader organisation - its bureaucrats and

its restrictions. The final aspect involved difficulties which arose from dealing with agents outside
of social services, such as doctors and court offi-
cials, problems which were seen to be inextricably
part of the public image of social work.

One strongly voiced minority interest (10 per
cent) highlighted the discrepancy between social
work training and social work practice. For these
people the match was a poor one: training had left
them ill equipped to cope with the job difficulties
that they had encountered.

Let us examine these points in more detail.


INSIDE THE OFFICE - ROLES AND RELATIONSHIPS


Load

The sheer quantity, and sometimes quality, of the
perceived work load was of particular significance:

> 'My main stresses come with too much work -
> can't look at it all, allocate it all - it
> starts building up. That's the time I feel
> most stressed, the time I'm most likely to
> take work home in my head.'

> 'Stress is an issue for me in terms of what
> demands are made of me, and by whom. I feel
> there are too many demands for me to meet
> despite the fact that I plan my work far more
> than I used to. I've been off sick for the
> last few days for this very reason.'

> 'My work stress comes from the massive volume
> of work and standards. My many activities
> demand an enormous time commitment, which
> really conflict with family requirements.'

There was a sense of desperation in trying to
maintain a semblance of control and competence in a
situation of increasingly unfavourable odds.

> 'The pressure comes from so many things to do
> at once. Can you do them all? Can you
> remember them all? You can't control this
> because it's demand from outside - from

clients. Sometimes I want to think about action while clients impatiently want a decision.'

'I have 27 clients - which is high for me as I'm just out of college. Time builds up stress. I plan my week with appointments, then things crop up. Kids running away from police, court reports and so on. This all builds up pressure on me. I have to then take work home, or get away somewhere to do it.'

Or finding enough hours in the day:

'When I do get exhausted it's from the straight demands of my case load. I get home late. And there's no way in the present system that you can really get to know your kids. Sometimes I'm out every night of the week - you just haven't enough time for any one kid. I have to do my report writing at home, usually during the morning. No way can you do this job in "normal" hours. If you're going to do a good job, it's part of your job - but it's all <u>very</u> trying. Stress in this job is no joke.'

'It's not just the quantity of work, it's the quality. There's just not enough time to do everything in the way I would like to. Because we have so much to do we have strict programmes which have got to be done, whatever. This is where I find the biggest stress. Much of the pressures are those over which I have no control. It's my responsibility to see that a client gets appropriate care, but I rely on others to respond to my requests. I have to check and nag colleagues. There's an awful lot of stress on me when I visit clients and nothing has been done - they take it out on me.'

Many would point a finger at the recording/paperwork features of their job. 'Real' social work, they felt, was not pushing pieces of paper around and compiling reports in triplicate. Yet the legal, local authority, and internal control system obliged them to do just this. It presented a fundamental conflict for those who had not the skills and/or

47

inclination to keep meticulous records, but who felt their prime duty was to be with their clients. This difficulty was exacerbated by the rather cramped, open-plan layout of the offices, offering little privacy to write uninterrupted.

'It's so easy to get behind with all the written work; this is when I really do feel stressed. Probably many social workers don't do half as many records as I do, and I do loathe writing! And there's just nowhere to do the writing here.'

'I work like mad, but I can't seem to catch up with myself. Masses of paperwork to do. Even my supervisor said she was unaware of the tremendous amount of work I had, while she pushes more work on me! I end up so aggrieved thinking there must be something wrong with me not being able to meet my work plans.'

'This morning I was sitting there by my desk with a huge pile of papers - there's an awful lot that needs doing at once, so I feel stressed. It's a question of not knowing what to do first leads to doing nothing.'

It also seemed that having a formal role as an organiser did not necessarily reduce the paperwork problems. The organisers of the home helps had their own stories to tell:

'We're responsible for so many people - nearly 200 at the moment, and 50 home helps to supervise. You're counselling home helps, seeing clients, dealing with all the nasties that go on. The sheer volume of work. It's always been like that. We're trying to visit 50 home helps once a month, plus clients once a month, plus do all the paperwork for the new referrals. There's no clerical support. In summer, you can have nine home helps off in one area, and you have to cover this. The stress just keeps building up with the load.'

'The paper work causes some degree of stress - we've virtually no clerical help. We carry 250 cases against a social worker's 40-50 - and that's an awful lot of paperwork. All

records have to be written up by hand. Every
new case we take on needs <u>twelve</u> pieces of
paper to start them. So you're sitting there
at night, 7.00pm, getting it all written up.
And we are publicly accountable so we have to
keep records.'

## Crises

Features of load were frequently expressed in terms
of handling crises. For some workers, deciding upon
the urgency of a particular request, and the appropriate action, was one of their most difficult tasks.
For example, a home help organiser recalls:

'Two weeks ago, a woman "needs home help" -
"bad back". On the back of the referral form
was the name of the doctor. To my mind,
there was no urgency, although she was elderly. I visited her home, but she wasn't in.
Back out there again on Friday and again she
wasn't in - she was at the surgery. I wrote
a letter saying another organiser would visit
on the following Tuesday. The woman dropped
dead on the Saturday.'

Social workers would feel torn as to where to put
their energies. A certain pattern of work had been
established, and they would then suddenly have to
turn rapidly to a new 'emergency'. A feeling arose
of constant sub-optimisation - the inability properly to finish, or progress, a job. But the human and
organisational costs of 'not doing something' could
be immense.

Yet, while crisis management was clearly an issue
for some social workers, it was those in supervisory
positions who were most articulate on this issue. A
senior social worker explains:

'There are delays constantly - and there are
always deadlines to meet in the job, which
you can't often meet. The chance of at least
one client blowing something pretty urgent is
fairly regular - at least one a week, sometimes twice. I think you shred yourself in
at least 50 different directions. Ever since
I've been here we haven't been fully staffed.
There's a very ambiguous expectation of

seniors. Not only will they do the job description, but all other bits as they occur -
such as covering the case load of someone off
sick. At one time I was covering two case
loads. One of my social workers was off four
months with a damaged spine, another was off
seven weeks of the same four months! It was
crippling for me. I wouldn't say I'm a per-
fectionist but I do like to do a proper job
for customers. But all I could do in that
time scale was to stick plaster on their
sores and run.'

Waves of crises were not unfamiliar to senior
staff. Ultimately, the team leader would find himself, or herself, confronted by their consequences:

'The worst times we're sitting here with a
stream of crisis cases happening. For
example, a couple of non accidental injuries,
and an old lady lying on the floor and the
doctor won't admit her to hospital. Also a
stream of people coming into Reception
downstairs, and staff demanding your attention. Christ!'

Supervision

Just over half of the group talked of their supervisor - a senior social worker, team leader, or a
main grade social worker for some social work assistants - as critical in absorbing, or failing to
absorb, stress. In an overloaded, ambiguous and
emotionally charged professional world, the supervisor could be the focus of stability. He or she
could be used to ventilate pent-up frustrations, to
test out client-related decisions, to seek political
advice, to review progress and prospects with continuing cases, or simply as a shoulder to cry on.
What, and how much, each social worker desired of
the supervisor depended upon that worker's personality, alternative sources of support, and his or her
perceptions of the supervisor.

Supervisory difficulties arose for a third of the
total group, for a number of different reasons.
Some were from an apparent mismatch of expectations,
and feeling wary of the supervisor:

'John, my supervisor, doesn't really provide
what I want. He tends to pick on things
which are important to him, not me. Excusing
or making excuses for other people all the
time. This irritates me and actually makes
me ill.'

'I don't get much supervision - I haven't
really got the supervision I require. I need
to get rid of the problems and tensions with
others. I need someone with time to listen
to me - it's a spiral.'

'Barry supervises me - well, I don't get
supervision. I don't get evaluation of cases
and of me. When I get a problem case, I grab
hold of Barry and force his attention - but
that's not supervision. What all this means
is that I'm not going to develop professionally unless I choose to read books.'

The above mentioned Barry was a team leader. He
was also a high flier in the organisation, having
already been offered a promotion in the forthcoming
re-organisation. He felt there was a lot of potential for building a strong team, but had backed-off
doing so because of the imminent split-up of the
group. His breadth of views on social work gave the
impression of a certain remoteness from the 'gutsy'
concerns of his supervisees:

'Supervision is attractive to me. Gives me a
chance to test my own ideas about social
work. I believe social workers should have a
wide range of skills, including case work.
But most social workers get hung up with, and
locked into, the case work alone, and the
relationship problems.'

There were some supervisors who were especially
sensitive to social workers in need of guidance and
support, and deeply resented having their attention
diverted from this work:

'Mixing clients and staff supervision is a
real conflict. There's real stress for me
when there are clients who need me and staff
who desperately need me - inexperienced
people struggling with exceedingly complex
issues. I have recently had to carry extra

case loads for absent social workers and
supervise four people - one of whom was behaving in the most unpleasant and unprofes-
sional manner you can envisage. Behaving
abominably, demanding more and more attention, like a spoilt child. That's when I
lose my temper and say I've had enough.'

Several social workers talked of forbidden areas
in supervision. A pattern had evolved where the
social worker would not talk about some of the most
threatening and sensitive difficulties because the
supervisor was seen to be part of them. For
example:

'I have regular meetings with my supervisor,
but always steer clear of my problems in
coping with my report work. Can I trust her?
I need her backing for my career progress,
but will she use this sort of thing as evidence against me? There are some painful
areas that are never discussed but need dis-
cussing so much. It's an awful dilemma for
me.'

Likewise, a supervisor could have 'blank spots',
especially if it concerned an evaluation of their
own competence:

'Supervision is new to me. It's OK, I
suppose, but I'm anxious - I'm never quite
sure whether I'm giving the people I'm supervising exactly what they are wanting. Do I
go into enough depth with them? Should I be
concentrating less on what they are doing and
more towards wider things? I'm really afraid
of what they will say about me, so I don't
ask. To be judged by a colleague is just too
much.'

The ultimate breakdown in the supervisory relationship was marked by a separation, usually (but
not always) initiated by the supervisee:

'I'm trying to find alternative supervision.
Currently I get supervised by the team leader
- but he's in a conflict situation between
being a manager and being my supervisor. I
get suspicious of his motives. He confuses
issues for me. So now I've not only got the

burden of doing the work but in deciding
priorities, which should be my supervisor's
role.'

'I just go my own way as my supervisor hasn't
been very helpful. He's firmly classed me as
someone with lots of experience, which <u>cer-
tainly</u> isn't <u>true</u>. So I do my own thing and
just tell him what I've been doing.'

'Although technically I'm supervised by Joe,
I soon found I couldn't stand his paternalistic style - and I told him this. He got very
hurt. He's a very kind man but he doesn't
question things in a way that suits me. So I
get my supervision and advice elsewhere.'

This last person speaking, Irene, in fact felt
little stress and was exceedingly single-minded in
her resolution. Her perception of her supervisor's
feelings matched his own views. In his words:

'My staff are my first priority, but with
some I go through so much stress. I go home
and worry. Irene, in particular, has found
support in the team she could not accept from
me. We had enormous difficulties, and this
really hurts.'

A supervisor's own stress was often contagious and
picked-up by the social worker in a number of different ways. It could thoroughly confuse a role relationship where strength and expertise were readily
attributed to the supervisor regardless. Indeed,
when a social worker felt in need of help, he or she
had little capacity or enthusiasm for taking on
board the supervisor's difficulties as well. One
social worker's ire at this was expressed as
follows:

'I've been very angry indeed with my supervisor because I feel I haven't been supported
properly. I haven't been getting the information I require. The messages I'm getting
from my supervisor are of the sort "don't be
too demanding". This supervision stress is
very difficult. I feel confused and lonely.'

She was aware that her supervisor had recently
failed to gain a promotion he desired. What she

seemed unaware of was the deep disappointment and
stress that this had caused him, which he had tried
to smother. He comments:

> 'People are a bit wary talking about how they
> feel, because they're not sure how I feel.
> They recognise that I've experienced a dis-
> appointment but won't talk about it. I don't
> go around getting angry about it or crying
> about it, therefore they're unsure how I will
> react to their feelings.'

The emotional imbalance in the supervisory relationship was accentuated when the social worker
became very dependent, possibly agressively so, on
the supervisor. This could be severely taxing for
the supervisor. Alan, a senior social worker, talks
about his supervision of Helen:

> 'I have so much stress from supervising
> Helen, much more than normal because she
> isn't as adequate as a fully trained social
> worker. As an assistant she shouldn't really
> be handling cases. But if she wasn't, she'd
> be upset, and what would I do with the cases?
> Others use me as a sponge. Perhaps I don't
> spread responsibility far enough. I seem to
> take on things which cause me stress.'

Helen, however, is bluntly uncompromising:

> 'I feel so desperate to have someone to take
> the problems to, and I depend on Alan for
> this. He criticises me for not bringing in
> any positives, but I tell him that's what
> he's there for! What I'm asking for is a pat
> on the head. He's paid to cope with my
> worries, poor sod. But if I haven't got him
> there, I'm going to go spare! He's been
> questioning this lately, which makes me very
> anxious.'

So for Helen, Alan's supervision is just what she
needs. Similarly for Judy:

> 'Alan is direct - you know where you are with
> him. He challenges me - I need that. He
> helps a little in the stress in dealing with
> kids. He helps me to feel a little less of a
> failure - gives me hope for the future.'

It seems, though, that Alan's effectiveness was achieved at considerable cost - to himself.

## Specialisms

While some members of the group were undertaking a type of social work for which they felt well-suited - working with children, adolescents, elderly, disabled, psychiatric, or some generic mix of these - others felt they were being prevented from 'doing their thing'. Sometimes this was because the natural flow of work into an office was of a particular type over which they could have little control. For example:

> 'I deal mostly with adolescents - more by the nature of the work in this office than by choice. There's little opportunity to do other work - although I'd so much like to.'

But at other times the roots of the difficulty appeared more political in nature - how a particular worker had been 'defined' by others, or the difficulty in influencing those who could bring about change:

> 'I'm qualified as a child care officer - and the powers that be think of me in those terms. I get pulled into meetings where such a representative is required. But I don't want to be seen in this way because I don't want to work with children all the time. There aren't the same sort of crises with the elderly. We don't move them to the four corners of the country, and they don't run away!'

> 'I've made a lot of moves in team meetings to say I don't want to take any more child care - I want more of the elderly, physically handicapped and psychiatric types. I've been asking and asking for this, and I never get it! Last week, in a team meeting, someone piped up and supported me; said it was ludicrous that I didn't get such cases when we need someone to do them. I chose Social Services because I didn't want to specialise for at least two to three years - and here I am specialising after one year.'

A number of social workers were more anxious about losing a way of working than seeking another. The fear that a decision in the office could take away something valued:

'Intake gives me variety, the possibility to focus on cases - especially the adolescent kids. It's where I'm happy. But for how long? What's going to happen next week, or in the next management move?'

Social work assistants

Rarely were social work assistants mentioned specifically by their organisational title. This seemed not because of their insignificance in the organisation, but because in practice their role was generally indistinguishable from that of the fully qualified social worker. This proved to be a paradoxical, and indeed stressful, position for the four social work assistants. They were not formally qualified social workers, were paid less than social workers, and technically de-barred from carrying the same responsibilities. Yet, in a resource-squeezed organisation, such distinctions were apt to become academic 'in order to keep the ship afloat'.

Reasons of organisational expediency for this state of affairs were usually appreciated by the social work assistants, but the residue it left with them was sometimes distasteful - they felt vulnerable and exploited:

'As a social work assistant here, you're at the bottom of the ladder. At times I've had to carry responsibility, such as office duty, with no one to back me. This is contrary to County policy, but there's no one else to do it! So you <u>are</u> obliged to do things like this, but I take the responsibility. So I will meet them on these crises, but will <u>they</u> back me? What I see, though, is that one minute they will <u>give</u> you this responsibility, but the moment you <u>assert</u> that responsibility, they hold back and reprimand you.'

'I try not to use the word "assistant" in case I'm seen as a "trouble maker", or someone pretending something I'm not. My work is very much like a social worker's, but I lack the right qualifications - which I really would like. But I've had so much trouble getting on a course. This would help me to develop professionally.'

Two of the assistants talked of their need to affirm their competence and also take extra precautions to protect themselves professionally:

'I feel I <u>can</u> do social work, rather than just "assisting" - I'd like nothing better than to be a qualified social worker. I sometimes feel I'm being put upon - exploited. On the whole, I do do social worker work, such as office duty, and strictly speaking I'm not allowed to receive kids into care, adoptions and mental health admissions. I probably shouldn't carry a case load. I really feel my lack of qualifications, so I need to write things down and check them frequently with my supervisor. Also, getting all my reports nicely tied up makes me feel competent and efficient. And if I'm inefficient, I'm only being a social work <u>assistant</u>!'

'I'm a social work assistant, but I do the same work as a social worker - I have my own case load. I find, as a social work assistant, that if I do anything wrong, it can affect the rest of my colleagues. This is quite a strain. I enjoy case work - I wouldn't have it any other way - but I have to make sure things are <u>doubly</u> tied, otherwise social workers will be got at if things go wrong. This is a bit of a bind - probably the worst area of my job. I go to my supervisor to tell her things I've done just to cover myself. There's no protected status for me as a social work assistant.'

## CLIENTS

As the social workers talked about their clients - which they did at some length - their descriptions revealed emotional knots which many of them found difficult, if not impossible, to loosen. While

terms such as 'caring for people', and 'being concerned for others', may be overworked, if not
stereotypical notions of social work, these were the
sentiments expressed by some. But difficulties
arose in steering the uncertain path between helping
a client and becoming part of his or her issues
through strong emotional involvement:

> 'In social work training we are told not to
> get too fond of our clients - "be profes-
> sional". We are supposed to protect the
> client by transferring the case. This doesn't
> do much about your feelings, though.'

Consequently, in practice, transferring a case was
a rare event. Involvement with the client was one
strong reason for this, but another was the admis-
sion of personal failure that it signified. It was
a public symbol of 'not managing professionally',
which some saw as more threatening than the difficulties posed by attachment to the client. So
clients tended to be 'owned', administratively and
psychologically.

One social worker's comments epitomise this phenomenon:

> 'I get protective feelings towards my clients
> if somebody here appears to be attacking
> them. I shouldn't let this confuse the goal
> of a meeting, so I suppress the feelings;
> this is stressful. Also, with clients it's
> so hard, and so important to decipher that
> part of the emotional response which comes
> from the effect of the client, and that part
> which comes from one's own biography - or the
> row with the wife last night. What can I do
> with these feelings?'

The protective feelings described by this man were
ones well recognised by many others, especially
those dealing with children. Children, it seemed,
touched some of the deeper sensibilities in social
workers, beyond the veneer of professional training.
For example:

> 'I get really emotionally involved if I see a
> child who's getting a raw deal. I've got an
> eleven-year-old boy in a children's home.
> He's smashing. I'd love to take him home

with me. His parents have deserted him, but he's got all sorts of fantasies and ideas about them. He stays in all weekend just in case they turn up. But they don't want to know. I have the incredibly painful task of continually pushing the reality into him. He will sob during interviews. That side of things really gets to me.'

'There's one case with which everyone says I'm emotionally involved. I don't disagree. I'm biased in her favour. Jean is a thir- teen-year-old who came into care - I was in at the beginning of her case which makes you more involved than a case which you take over. You're there at the crisis - crying, arms around her. Jean was thrown out of her home by her step-father, who's a right bas- tard - horrible. Constant rejection - chil- dren's home, home to Dad which didn't work, foster family with possibility of indecent assault by foster father, children's home again, but they couldn't cope after two weeks.'

There was little indication that social workers considered these feelings to be professionally in- appropriate. Quite the contrary. The view was expressed that a good relationship with a client was inevitably a close one, and some clients they would feel closer to than others. The problems arose in managing the effects of the relationship:

'Emotionally, I've enough child care to cope with - perhaps I'm not very strong, but I find child care quite wearing. If it wasn't for the emotional side of the job, the administrative side wouldn't be difficult. Some kids you like more than others. One of my lads is so sweet, and a rogue, he's very endearing - I could take him home with me! When you make a decision about someone like that to go to a residential school and he then comes in to see you and tells you how awful it is and how he's getting hit about at school - what do you do? He could be making it up, but basically he's crying out for love. Have you made the right decision? The emotion is very difficult to cope with. This reaction has to happen. You have to get

close to have a good relationship. The kid
doesn't know how I feel - you can't tell him
your feelings. Maybe that's why it's difficult to cope with.'

Behind such attachments lay many factors. At one
layer, professional competence and self image were
client-bound, so there was almost an inevitable
encapsulation of the client, reinforced by the one-
to-one nature of the professional contact and the
lack of support felt by some social workers. The
focus on the client therefore intensified. At
another level some clients reflected part of the
social worker's biography - perhaps rather vulnerable parts. There was talk of their own desire for
children, or regret at their children growing up.
Others saw their own child-rearing or childhood
difficulties mirrored in the client. Some were
particularly sensitive to the consequences of
marriage difficulties because of their own marital
problems. Overwriting all of these factors was, for
some, the ethic of concern for the underdog, the
vulnerable. Clearly children, especially small
children, would appear as most in need of help and
protection. Yet the vagaries of personal attachment
confused even this:

'One lad is so withdrawn I can't talk to him.
Hunches up in the furthest corner of the car
- just answers "yes" and "no". I feel I
should be working much harder with him - but
I know I haven't the resources - others would
suffer. It gets even more complicated because I probably avoid contact because I
don't enjoy seeing him - this makes me feel
guilty.'

Caring appears a fickle notion in practice. Its
boundaries reflect more basic, less controllable,
emotional factors not easily overridden by acquired
skills. As one social worker observed:

'Commitment to a case is more than a straight
professional decision; it's a decision which
you are directly tied up in. Some kids you
really like - you can identify with them.'

And as another described, with warmth and affection:

60

'Some of the kids are gorgeous. Two I've got
- tiny things because they've always been
deprived, I always bring them a bar of choco-
late. I buy mum one as well because she gets
ever so upset if she hasn't got one. She's
just a child, you see. Some dads are like
this now - it's children with children. It's
a parenting role for me.'

The paradox of involvement did not escape the
social worker's attention. On the one hand, went
the argument, attachment and involvement were professionally desirable, an inevitable human quality,
and personally rewarding for social worker and
client. On the other hand, certain attachments can
befuddle thinking, be very stressful for the social
worker who needs to maintain some social distance
from the client (there are many clients to deal
with), can confuse the client who is being coun-
selled towards self-help, and can make separation a
mutually painful affair. So the social worker walks
an emotional tightrope, entering people's lives,
mixing parts of them with his or her own life, and
trying to use that mix to act professionally for the
client. Perhaps inevitably the balance cannot
always be maintained, ultimately to the cost of the
social worker, and sometimes to the client's detri-
ment.

Dependence and counterdependence

One feature of a close and emotionally intense relationship with a client is that the client can come
to depend on the social worker for help and action.
This, according to certain codes of social work
practice, is to be avoided in that the client should
be helped towards self-reliance, the social worker
ultimately becoming dispensable in the relationship.

Such tenets were amongst the guiding principles of
supervisory sessions, and were well known to the
social workers. Yet in practice, the theory was not
always easy to apply. Certainly, some social workers appeared very deliberate in enacting their
roles with clients, and more than alert to dependence issues. As one remarked:

'I try not to create dependency, so I watch
the <u>timing</u> of my moving in and out of a

61

situation. Most people seem to want to <u>keep</u> clients - I don't.'

For others, though, reducing dependency was less a professional principle and more a matter of removing a personal irritation or threat:

'This mother is a terribly depressing character - almost whining. She'd like to depend on me, but I've more or less closed her case because I wasn't going to have this. She's been such a burden to me. She says her kids are too much for her - "take them off me - they're in my way". She dislikes her older kids - perhaps that's why I don't like her; <u>I</u> have difficulties with older kids and she's trying to push them on me - something <u>I</u> can't handle. Yet I'm the one who's supposed to know everything!'

But often dependency would catch the social worker unawares - not noticed until some significant break in routine:

'The dependency of some clients on me is sometimes frightening. For example, when I got back from my last holiday, some gave the impression I'd been away for years! They would say "I knew you were going away, but I didn't realise you wouldn't be <u>there</u>!" With some clients I have to be very careful about telling them I'll be away because the shock would be too great for them.'

At other times, the hook of a dependent relationship was recognised, but the social worker felt helpless to remove it:

'Sometimes if I don't see a particular kid, I fear he'll think I'm letting him down - so I keep going on.'

'There are quite a lot of peaks of anxiety, especially when I know people are very dependent on me. So if I don't do something for them, nothing will happen. Their dependency has a certain power over me - can nag me and make me feel very guilty.'

There was a double-bind inherent in the 'client shouldn't be dependent but I can't let go' syndrome. It was felt to be undesirable to prolong a relationship with certain clients, but to stop work with a client risked losing a rewarding relationship and letting the person down. As one team leader noted:

'It's the "letting go" which can be so tough. Some social workers can't let go, although the situation seems OK, they want to stay around "in case". Social workers can end up dependent on their clients.'

And it was at this point of counterdependency - the social worker being dependent upon their clients - that the relationship becomes particularly problematic. The social worker may find the client so unusually rewarding that, almost unconsciously, the relationship is prolonged:

'I have a woman who wants to depend on me and I've been working to get her out of that. But what I now realise is that I've colluded in this because she's the only nice client in my case load - the only person who does exactly what I want her to do!'

The rewards of counterdependency may reflect the social worker's deeper personal desires, such as for affection and security:

'My care for the kids brings me a lot of stress. I like kids - I love kids. Most of the kids like me. They get very important to me, perhaps too important. I guess I just need to be needed. Small kids especially give you a lovely feeling. Rush up to you. Put their arms around you. And when things are going wrong for them, I suppose I feel as upset as they do.'

So, for these social workers, to 'let go' of a client was often very much more than a detached professional decision. It meant relinquishing something of themselves which was not always a simple matter to confront.

Responsibility for others

The social worker's brief of responsibility is considerable. In terms of the Social Services Department's own public literature:

> 'We provide social care for those in need.
> We protect families and individuals who are
> at risk, whether it be an elderly person
> living in an unheated home or a child who is
> ill-treated by his parents.'

A statutory backing to this remit gives social workers the power to recommend a care order for a child, arrange fostering and adoption, organise domiciliary services, pay money to a family in an emergency, move an old person to a supportive home or institution if he or she cannot manage alone, and provide hostels for the mentally handicapped. Acting 'responsibly' for the client within these powers weighed heavily upon the social workers' shoulders, a burden aggravated by the feeling that they were never quite their own professional masters. Above them was a line of accountability from team leader through to senior management, and from senior management to local government members and the general public. Such delegated power provide an important check on the use and abuse of the social worker's power, but it also eroded feelings of professional confidence and worth. The trail of accountability could sometimes leave clients feeling as confused and helpless as the social worker, as one worker recalls in the following anecdote:

> 'I was told I had to cut down visiting hours
> because of current time-per-client availability. To try and explain to the client the
> reasons behind this, especially when I'm not
> too sure myself, can be a problem. Administrative arguments look meaningless to the
> client. I tried this once and it rebounded
> on me. I had to cut an old lady from 15 to
> 10 hours, then 10 hours to six hours. She
> kept asking why I was doing it. I kept
> giving her logical explanations. Eventually
> we ended up in laying accountability on
> Maggie Thatcher. She said she'd write to
> Maggie Thatcher, and she did! Went up to
> Parliamentary Secretary for Social Services
> then back to the Director and then to me! So
> I had to write back. When I saw her she said
> - "Well, didn't do much good writing to her -
> you answered!".'

In meeting their responsibilities, the social workers were anything but dispassionate 'people processors'. There was an image presented of agonising over decisions, and anguish over the possible consequences. Few out of the whole group felt comfortable with a personal decision that appeared to affect fundamentally the early course of an individual's life in directions indeterminate - no matter how right it seemed for the circumstances at the time:

'Stress for me involves making certain decisions and the responsibility it entails. Like taking a child into care, or whether a child should stay with or go back to foster parents. It's uppermost in my mind at the moment! It's my name on the bit of paper - my decision produces the fate of that child over so many years. Is it going to be right in one year, or five year's time? Once a Care Order is made the County Council are loath to go back on that. Is this totally unrealistic? It certainly emotionally upsets me - puts me under stress. I get emotional because the kids mean a lot to me.'

'I have to make critical decisions on the fostering of a child. It is often a terrible decision to make about a child's life. It can give you nightmares - a decision on a one-year-old that they should never go home! Have I made the right decision?'

'Do you know that even with the backing of your superiors, you're still left unsure that you're making the right decision. The stress comes from the fact that maybe someone is going to be damaged if you've made the wrong decision.'

Participants frequently pointed out how their work provided them with a constant reminder of their professional fallibility - there were no certainties when making prognostications about a client. What was certain, they felt, was that if they did not act for a client, the client could get worse, so something had to be done. On the other hand the long-term effects of some of their interventions were so hard to judge, would they end up harming the client? So either way left them with worries about others'

futures and their role in them; few were sufficiently alienated from their clients to think otherwise:

'I have really worried about the problems
left over by Friday afternoon. It's worrying
because it is people I'm dealing with, not
goods standing in a half-finished state of
manufacture. There's that awful stress from
this - from having to get it all done.'

'The fostering business affects me most.
Separation and loss really gets to me - I'm
in the middle, making decisions. What are we
doing to children in foster homes if we don't
have better resources? It is very stressful.'

'As a social worker, your feelings about
events are part of your work. So much is
subjective. Why should I feel that a baby
should be taken into care, or a child put
into an assessment centre? Also, there's an
awful lot of anguish and emotion floating
around to cope with: people shouting at me.
People are very angry with you and rightly so
- they should be. You're taking their children away, as they see it.'

'I'm fairly new to the job - working with the
deaf. My job is aiming to change, with
people's consent, something in their life and
relationships. But I haven't got this with
deaf people. I might know where I want them
to go, but I'm buggered if I know how I'm
going to get there. The usual lines of communication don't work. Oblique meanings
aren't there. They find it difficult to
expose feelings. You learn to cope with
experience - but it's bloody frustrating
to sit there and wait for experience. On the
way, people are going to suffer because you
haven't the experience.'

Children at risk

The most sensitive client situation, mentioned by
almost everyone, concerned children at risk - reported evidence of a child who had been, or may be,
physically abused or injured. Here, the social
worker, and indeed the whole agency, was most liable

to public scrutiny should things go wrong. It pressed the system into top gear, so the social worker was under little illusion as to the priority of the demand. Furthermore, the abused child could stimulate the most protective of feelings in the social workers.

Two senior social workers made their views on this position quite clear:

> 'I'm not a worrier by nature, I don't worry about being incompetent about things that aren't important by my selection. If the reports were here up to the ceiling, that wouldn't disturb me unduly because, in the fullness of time, I'd take care of that. But when I know we've got four very small kids at severe risk on those two caseloads of the social workers who are absent or sick - that's anxiety.'

> 'I'm aware there's a basket with "at risk" situations in them which has to be looked at - that's stressful because I feel I <u>have</u> to take action. What happens if something goes wrong? Have I caused it myself? Have I taken too much responsibility? Have I missed something?'

One fairly hard-bitten social worker was more than a little jittery in 'non-accidental injury' cases:

> 'They are probably the most emotive we can get involved with. While these cases can bring the most satisfaction if you can do the right thing for the child, I'd really prefer not to deal with them. One of the few client situations that can get to me.'

There were some child-at-risk cases which social workers felt placed them in impossible situations. In protecting the child they could end up harming the parents and also subjecting the child to a significant separation trauma. On the other hand in taking no action they risked other damage to the child and a public pillorying. In their view, they could not win.

# Danger and deception

Threat from clients could be directly physical in nature, as well as psychological. Not often were the social workers intimidated in this way, but when they were (reported by four people), the experience was usually a memorable one. These are the recollections from two social workers:

> 'I went out to see this bloke with a colleague ... a terrifying experience. He was a very frightening man. He locked us in his room. I thought, Christ, ten years ago I could have coped with this easily, but now I can't. At the time I thought I wouldn't get out alive - he talked about poisoning people and then went off to make us a cup of tea! All a bit heavy!'

> 'I had to go to London with another social worker to pick up a baby at risk. A girl we had in care had run away with the baby. We found the girl in a squat with a couple of West Indian girls and a cousin. When I climbed in the window I didn't know what to expect. I was prepared for the worst. The other social worker found it extraordinary, the risk I was taking - but you always take risks just knocking on a door! The person may be bonkers, or drunk, or come at you with a knife. I've nearly had my teeth knocked down my throat a couple of times.'

Not infrequently a social worker was cornered into a position where doing something in the 'client's best interest' was directly incompatible with what the client wanted. In such cases some compromise may be sought, or the client may be gently persuaded, over time, to the social worker's point of view. While the social worker had a certain professional authority (and often desired to exercise it to affirm his or her role) notions of 'honesty', 'trust', and 'client free-will' were implicit ground-rules in the social worker-client interaction. Blatant deception was not. But sometimes deception indeed occurred; for example:

> 'An old lady may not be able to look after herself any longer, and her relatives are run into the ground trying to manage her. She

doesn't want to go into a home - but you feel it's in her best interests. But you are doing it against her will. I find this <u>very</u> hard to come to terms with - but there are often no options. The old ladies are lied to - they're not often aware they are going into an old people's home - they are losing their own home.'

In this particular case, the social worker rationalised that 'normally they are happier in the end in the home'. Nevertheless, the decision left her uncomfortably boxed-in. Others reflected similarly when they found themselves telling less than the truth to a client as 'the only way of helping that person in the end'.


## THE ELUSIVENESS OF SUCCESS

Success for a social worker was generally a delight, an occasion to be savoured and remembered - because of its rarity. They talked of 'odd periods when things come together', the 'very occasional times when you feel that something you've done is really going to make a difference', 'getting kicked in the teeth 100 times, but it's the 101st time, when you've got through, that it's great'.

In dispassionate moments the social workers would reflect that their generally unrewarding client-work was an inevitable fact of social work, given the complexity of individual lives. Yet few who chose to talk in detail about this left doubts as to how wearisome it was. It challenged the very validity of their professional existence, and demanded a massive pool of energy to simply keep going. Those who did not feel this way were predisposed to see a silver lining in any intervention, or were able to tolerate long periods before reaping rewards. Others could avoid the issue by dealing with specific short-term difficulties, where some immediate results of action were observable - a stance viewed with circumspection by one senior worker:

'It's very easy to feel discouraged about one's purpose and role. Ironically, most of the encouragement is given to social workers for the things they've contributed to least. A quick solution involving little skill or expertise often brings the most appreciation from the client. It looks an excellent service to these clients, but can be professionally least consequential to the social worker.'

Why some found success so elusive is traceable to a number of factors. The first concerns deep uncertainty about the wisdom of certain interventions, and confusion over the proper signs of success:

'And how do we know we're right? That's the frightening bit - have I made the right decision? This is one of the things that tires you out. Your time is so limited. You can get so many feelings of doubt - you can get too many of these feelings.'

'In this job you never know whether you've done anything right - especially with kids. How can you decide that the decision you've made (albeit with other people) is the right one? You don't know until that child is grown up. The choices are more clear cut with the elderly - you can see the results when you put in a home help for an old person, or move an old person from a grotty house to a decent one. But with children and teenagers you just don't know. Maybe some initial improvement, and then it will go back. It's like families which keep cropping up. Same problems year after year. You think you've solved the problems - but you haven't really.'

Added to such self doubts were discouraging comments from the clients themselves. Even fairly thick skinned social workers were pained at being 'thanked' by their client with a reminder that they were being paid to help out; or finding that their success with a child was sharply denigrated by that child's parents:

'The parents seem to want you to fail, and are not happy until you do. They're angry if you succeed and they rarely will accept success in our terms. They construe our success as failure. This is draining - you can't win.'

The lonely social worker had yet further difficulties. Several talked of their need to explore and
discover their degree of success with a colleague or
superior, but could find no-one to fit this role
adequately.

There were certain types of client who acted as a
focus for the social worker's feelings of helplessness or failure - the 'intractables'. These
were people for whom nothing seemed to work or could
be done. They could depress a social worker who
already felt trapped by the desire to 'keep trying'.
Some senior staff saw this as a problem of misplaced
invincibility - in the words of one team leader:

> 'Sometimes the problem is getting social
> workers to stop believing they have magic
> wands. For example this morning we had a
> case conference where a social worker was
> having to confront the fact that a family
> would have nothing to do with social workers.
> We have no magic ways of making them co-
> operate so we simply cannot work there - even
> if it's a case of non-accidental injury. I
> have to get social workers to accept this -
> it's not their failure.'

Another took a similar line, but with rather more
identification with the social worker:

> 'The staff sometimes have to see they can
> help some people but not others - quite a
> conflict for me sometimes. For example we
> have an old lady who has 18 dogs, all thin.
> There are rats in the house and she's been
> bitten by the rats and the dogs. It's the
> second house the Housing Department have put
> her in, and I'm being asked what I'm going to
> do. But I can't do anything. The RSPCA have
> got rid of most of the dogs now, but the
> doctor says she's fit mentally and physically
> and she says she wishes to live in that
> state. But we're left with the feeling that
> there's an old lady who desperately needs
> some kind of help. But we just have to wait
> for a crisis before we can act - until she's
> ill and admitted to hospital. I have to go
> logically through the options with my social
> worker or home help with this - some awful
> choices to make.'

The entrapment with the hopeless client took on
different complexions with different workers. One
saw it as an inevitable consequence of misplaced
resources - 'Like paying £100 a week to put a kid
into care when this money could have got his mum out
of queer street'. For another, taking on a mother
who had rejected her children represented a maso-
chistic reflection of that social worker's inability
to cope with her own children - 'How do you get a
mother and son to relate differently - I don't
know.' And still others expressed a general confusion and exasperation with a client:

'This woman's psychiatric - you can't do
anything. She just sits there and abuses.
She's got me so low - I just dread knocking
on her door.'


ORGANISATIONAL INFLUENCES

Most of the job features which touched a social
worker's life had a locally perceived source. But
some elements were seen to emanate from the wider
organisation - the 'bureaucracy' and 'headquarters'.
While the blueprint for social work bureaucracy has
an enabling rationale, offering services and support
to the social worker (or more abstractly to the
'social work task'), it was far from universally
received in this way. This was hinted at in the
pilot study described earlier, and it was clearly a
politically sensitive issue judging by the Director's desire not to tackle it as a specific part of
the study. Nevertheless it re-emerged in various
forms in the social workers' reflections and
stresses. The sentiments expressed by the following
two social workers were typical of those of approximately one third of their colleagues:

'Social work cannot go on without an organisational scaffolding. I regard lots of
structures as potentially helpful - but they
must be live and responsive. Sometimes
there's an awful mismatch between the social
work task and the administrative edifice
deemed necessary to protect the organisation.
These are the things I find most depressing.
Overwieldy review panels for the handicapped;
bureaucrats rationing procedures which get in
the way. Also, there are the expectations of

72

HQ advisers' skills and knowledge which aren't forthcoming. That's a terrible let down.'

'There's a very hierarchical system here which I have difficulty fitting into; I <u>try</u> to pretend it doesn't exist. That's where the stress occurs - when I have to encounter the fact that it <u>is</u> a hierarchy. Working here involves an enormous sweat - right forms at the right time in the right order. Transfer slips are supposed to be filled in for every kid moved, but you've got dozens going home weekends, so you avoid this. You do your best to bypass these systems - informal arrangements. There are people in HQ on the end of a phone who I've never seen.'

Social workers felt constricted when trying to 'work with the bureaucracy'. Appropriate profes- sional decisions on clients, based on knowledge from much face to face contact, often had to be reshaped, sometimes radically, to meet the requirements of the organisational bureaucracy - which frequently felt unresponsive, and altogether unattuned to 'face work':

'Look, I've just made a careful decision on placing a kid with some foster parents - it <u>feels</u> right for the girl. But I'm so worried about what's going to be said to me by the Department hierarchy, because it's not their decision. I felt theirs was wrong. I <u>know</u> <u>my</u> <u>client</u> and I'm going to end up with <u>five</u> people saying I haven't the right to make the decision I have done.'

'It's so frustrating. At times I've taken action in the best interests of a client which has been blocked by bureaucratic action - or I've been making demands on the wrong budget at the wrong time. I give up in these circumstances. I can sympathise with those who say you can't do proper social work in a local authority.'

Few social workers found it easy or comfortable to think in bureaucratic terms. Most were client- centred in their concerns and skills which, together with their office problems, left them little surplus

energy to devote to tackling a 'faceless bureaucracy'. And faceless was how it could appear, reinforced by its apparent failure in times of need:

'Sometimes you receive a crisis call and you
feel the need to call for some advice from
HQ. I ring up, leave messages, but no-one
calls back. Meanwhile the case is ongoing
and time is passing while you're trying to
contact the person who actually makes the
decision. Often they feel so distant. In
practice I can often act without them -
through, for example, negotiating directly
with Children's Homes for a place. I know
the people there and it's my client. But
County Hall complicate all this. I feel I
have to fight the hierarchy - someone has to
countersign everything.'

'I'm absolutely desperate for a very special
place for a kid who has deep problems. HQ
are absolutely useless. There are specia-
lists there who are supposed to have
resources, and all they do is throw it back
at you! I'm fed up trying. He'll probably
end up in prison if we can't find something
for him.'

Such frustration was not confined to the main
grade social workers. One team leader came close to
rage when talking about his relations with headquarters:

'Nobody in the headquarters sees the pressure
here; nobody wants to see it! They just
don't seem to understand that we can't keep
piling on more cases for social workers -
they'll stop functioning. The fact that we
have no more time left to cope is denied by
HQ. I'm in a Catch 22 situation.'

Certain social workers would circumnavigate some
of these difficulties by ignoring procedures in
order to get the job done, cultivate sympathetic
contacts within the organisational system and develop informal relationships with key personnel outside the organisation whom they knew they could rely
upon. Thus they became quite sophisticated and
political in their work, which seemed one recipe for
survival. But this could leave them with feelings of

guilt and anger because it was a use of time that
they basically resented.


## THE WORLD OUTSIDE

Typically, the social worker is not dealing with a
client in professional isolation; there are other
agents and agencies outside the organisation which
impinge, such as medical practitioners, hospitals,
residential homes, the police, magistrates, and the
Social Security Department. All claim certain
rights over the client which may be in direct conflict with the social worker's intentions. Moreover, the 'world outside' views social work with
some circumspection, closely observing how it meets
some of its obligations. Let us examine these areas
in a little more detail.

Image of social work

> 'We're a bit like a dustbin taking in
> everyone's social garbage. And that's how we
> are treated.'

> 'Social work covers so many functions, a
> large part of it is the "dumping off" bit -
> the dustbin of the social services. People
> avoid their societal responsibilities, such
> as the elderly dying of hypothermia, battered
> children. There's an expectation that if
> these are referred to social services then
> anyone else can be relieved of responsibi-
> lity. We're appalling at public relations -
> few know who we are or what we are. I've
> polled some local streets - few knew what we
> do. Aids and 'phones - some dim awareness.
> But there was much confusion - particularly
> with Social Security.'

The feeling of being in a low status profession,
picking up society's human debris, was an oft re-
peated sentiment. It caused anguish in different
ways. Ideologically it was offensive to some social
workers as it reinforced the lack of caring that
exists naturally within a community. These people
wished to view themselves as part of a resource
network, fostering community self help - not as a
separated group of first-aiders or trouble shooters.
Others could live with their 'outsider' role, but

resented the lack of appreciation of the demands and difficulties of their position. A few, like the social worker quoted above, conceded that they might be their own worst enemies in this respect as they provided little effective public relations from within the profession.

The most pessimistic saw no hope for a shift in public attitudes towards their work, particularly recalling the negligible impact of their recent industrial action. They pointed out how frequently 'the public' were only too happy to forget about the less fortunate in society, and ignore the people who chose to care for the 'needy' - except when the service was removed or some disaster occurred. Also, a political climate which resisted social services' expenditure, and encouraged mainly the 'active' and 'productive' people in society, could hardly help their cause.

The hard edge of social work was seen as the most visible - such as when moving children and old people into care. This could result in an ogreish image for the social worker:

'Most professions don't look upon social workers as being very important, so we've got to build our own egos and importance. The reputation we have in this Area is "taking the kids away" - that's how they see you. It's worrying because it's not what we should be doing - I really feel this. It's quite a thing to carry. I'd so much like us to be seen as people who don't just take the kids away or put people into homes. Some we leave at their home because they want this. They want to die in their own place, despite squalor, rats, filth or whatever. We only Section people if they really are a danger to themselves or to other people. But we've all sometimes signed a Section, or refused to, and wondered whether we're right. We're not very good managers - but that's not what we're here for.'

The generalised feeling of being underrated found focus on particular agencies, some of which were seen to react as if threatened by the social worker. Typical descriptions cited the Department of Health and Social Security as responding to 'just another bloody social worker'; the police viewing social workers as 'soft, namby pambies'; and magistrates disliking social workers because they robbed them of some of their power. Certainly court-work high-lighted a struggle for recognition:

'Court work I look upon at best as a bit unpleasant. Our relationship with the court has been strained for some years. Usually the court work is based on a complaint or conflict - rarely is my role one where the court recognises the validity of my exis-tence.'

'If I do a late visit I find it very diffi-cult to shut off. If I finish about 5.00pm I can forget about it until next day - <u>unless</u> it's a court case. I definitely worry about this the night before - how to maintain credibility.'


WHO DEFINES THE PROBLEMS?

One facet of the social worker's interaction, and status, with other professionals is a jockeying for position in 'diagnosis' of a client. The social worker's view of a client's difficulties could be very different from the doctor's, medical consul-tant's, psychiatrist's, or some other interested party. There could then follow a contest of power, and often an ill-matched one at that. A case illus-trates:

'My work with the elderly can be really stressful because I'm having to co-ordinate with the hospitals and doctors who won't define certain people as medically ill - they insist on them having social problems when they definitely haven't. I've a case in point now. A poor man who wanted to go into one of our houses. Lived alone all his life. Suffered with a nervous eczema type com-plaint. He started to get rather anxious. His GP felt he should get day care - get a good meal each day. We did our part - filled in forms, and so on. When it came to telling the old man the vacancy was there, he just didn't want to go. You can't force them to

go, so he remained at home, but he deterio-
rated fast. He wasn't eating. Meals on
wheels came, but we found a table of mouldy
food when we visited him - he hadn't touched
the food. I took off his sock as he was
scratching so much. What met my gaze horri-
fied me. Lots of black ulcers looking as if
they were gangrenous. I phoned the doctor
immediately saying he must be admitted for
treatment. But the surgery said the doctor
had given him cream to use. Yes, there was a
shelf full of cream. But he hadn't used it.
He hadn't bathed or washed. He'd lost interest in everything. He'd become very confused. The doctor had brought a psychiatrist
to him, but the psychiatrist said he wasn't a
psychiatric case. The doctor said he was a
social case, not a medical one, so he didn't
require a medical bed.

In the end we had to make a stand. In fact a
private home which has recently opened took
him in. He was so bad they had to segregate
him from the rest. He couldn't stand - skin
falling off him. In the end, after an enormous battle, we managed to get him into hospital. That destroys relationships,
especially with the private home. They
couldn't cope. This has happened on several
occasions. I do know the pressures they are
under, but it's funny how a bed can be found
when you press hard enough. I have to get my
team leader to support me. This is stress
for me. I get psychological reactions. I
feel so useless and helpless in these situations.'

This example highlights the sometimes grossly
differing definitions of a client's condition, with
the client caught somewhere between contestants for
the 'right' definition. A similar scenario was
observed with other professionals - such as between
two consultants, or a consultant and a GP. Few
social workers had much appetite, or skill, for such
politicking; they talked of being fast ground down
by the events.

The social workers' uncertainties in these con-
tests could linger and nag at their confidence:

'One night a particular woman was prepared to
go into hospital, but the hospital refused to
take her unless it was legally ratified -
because in the past she had refused to stay
in hospital to undergo treatment. So I was
persuaded to sign a Section by the GP. I
worried about it for days. I felt inexperienced and pressurised by medical men and I
was a bit out of my depth. Sometimes you get
a lot of hustling from other agencies - such
as pressure to put a child into care from
parents, police or school. Am I making the
right decision when all these other people
think that something else should be done?
Have I done it right?'

'It's other agencies that get to me, not the
clients. A few weeks ago I was asked to find
a weekend foster home for a girl at a residential school who had threatened to kill her
mum. After I talked about it with her
father, who wanted her home, I agreed that it
would be OK if she went home. Then everything exploded. The Education Department and
Child Guidance were in dismay. The head-
master of the school said he'd have to bring
her home himself with two escorts. The pressure on me was enormous. Had I made the
right decision? Done the right thing? That
was dreadful. Deep doubt. I physically felt
the pressure. That's stress for me.'

VULNERABILITY

There were many accounts depicting social workers
constantly glancing over their shoulders, checking
they were 'covered', guarding against the catastrophe that could attract public attention:

'There's always the worry about what I've
done with my clients because disaster stories
abound in our trade. The press are always
around, pressurising.'

'We had a near public inquiry about an elderly gentleman dying. It alerts us all. Are
we doing our work properly? Are we covering
ourselves? Are we getting it all down on

paper? Stress gets to everyone in these circumstances.'

The consciousness of their vulnerability to stricture through legal sanctions and press inquiry was sometimes translated into fear, and elaborate self-protection:

'I can put a lot of work into getting all clients cared for for a weekend. But sometimes a letter doesn't get through and all havoc lets loose. If an old lady is found dead on the floor on Monday morning, everyone would be shouting, "What's gone wrong?" And the finger points at me. This terrifies me.'

'Sometimes this department goes crazy to cover itself - to look right to outsiders. The other day I was told by management that I had to get a particular place for a lad. He didn't actually need our care and protection - it was a political move. In fact I found him a place and he refused to go! He then kept absconding. I was told I had to keep him there - force him to attend each morning. The department wanted to cover itself. I had to find all sorts of ways of keeping him there - such a waste of time!'

Those who had actually experienced being in the limelight of a public inquiry described the pain of their memories, and their heightened sensitivity to future possible errors or miscalculations. They would find themselves spending an inordinate amount of time checking and cross-checking their records, and still not resting easily when they had got home. Their experiences emerged as part of the common knowledge and wisdom of an office. As one team leader noted, few observers were particularly generous or forgiving when looking at a social worker's activities. The dramatic failures were remembered, hanging like a noose about their necks.


TRAINING

' "Youth cultures" and "Marxism" go down the pan here. My social work course, the CQSW, did not prepare me for the nitty gritty of the work here. I really feel bitter about

80

the courses I've been on - seem to have <u>no</u> relationship to what actually goes on here. I'm simply trying to survive now, and I feel I should have come out of my training with more than just a pretty bit of paper.'

Such embittered reactions to the adequacy of training were to be found amongst a number of young, newly qualified social workers. They talked of the shock of working in a bureaucracy with its 'bits of paper' and 'hierarchy', and taking on a very large case load very soon after joining the department.

Three areas of training came in for particular criticism. The first was that the pace and 'space' of qualifying training was grossly out of proportion to the demands of the actual job. Students, it was claimed, were introduced to the administrative aspects of social work during training, but, in the words of one social worker, 'had all the time in the world to do it'. Similarly, the small number of clients during student days permitted the development of close relationships which seemed impossible when the client load was high. Secondly, the training appeared politically naive, with little appreciation being gained about the tussles of organisational life in a social services department. Training placements were seen as inadequate in this respect because they often afforded the student a fairly protected status. Finally, few felt prepared for the business of personal survival in social work - which required more knowledge and skills about the psychological and physical demands of client and organisational pressures. Training, it was felt, should directly address these issues.

More experienced social workers talked about their own training in similar terms, some adding the particular problems of early specialisms. One senior remarked as follows:

'When you've trained in something you know exactly how to go about things. That's how it's been for me with the elderly. But the real pressures come when you have to do work that you're untrained for. I find that I'm sometimes working in the dark with court work, conferences on children and even problem families.'

81

Another found his recent retraining confusing because of the 'dozens of different models now being offered'. This, he felt, led to conflict of practice. Indeed, an erstwhile training officer, now a senior social worker, viewed this as one ingredient in 'spreading training so thinly that it is almost useless'.

So, for a small proportion of participants, particularly the recently qualified, pre-employment training provided little protection against the stress of 'real' work. Some of their difficulties were no doubt aggravated by the circumstances of their joining the department - such as during times of crisis, or high absenteeism. Inadequate organisational bridging between training and the job was described by some - few induction procedures and little support or supervision.

I gained the impression that the experiences of organisational life soon shaped learning and attitudes in ways which overlayed, if not obliterated, memories of initial training. Yet the early days were crucial ones for the novitiate, when the quality of training could make the difference between coping and not coping with certain threats.

# 6 Interface with non-work

Up until now we have regarded personal reactions at work as influenced mainly by job experiences. But, like any other worker, a social worker has a non-work life which may be emotionally demanding. In such circumstances, are threat and stress at work more likely to occur? Do social workers have special coping skills, perhaps being able to psychologically segment portions of their lives? Where, if at all, do work and non-work influences interact?

The evidence suggests that when social workers find non-work (usually home) difficulties beginning to sap their emotional energies, this very soon reflects on their work feelings and performance. In what appears as an emotionally taxing job little spare energy is left to direct to out-of-work problems. The end-of-day exhaustion (described in Chapter 4) left many feeling 'empty', so home relationships, which required their attention, could suffer. This in turn could further reduce their tolerance of, and resistance to, work pressures. Few social workers in this group possessed extraordinary coping skills which could assist them in managing beyond the already heightened emotional demands of the job. As one senior stated, with firm conviction:

'I couldn't continue in this job unless I had a stable family grouping of my own. I couldn't cope with the home pressures <u>plus</u> work pressures.'

And indeed, his affirmation was well in tune with those who had to contend with the double sets of pressures. For example:

'My mother had a brain tumour after Christmas - gave us a mass of problems. At that time I found it difficult to do my job, although I can usually switch off home when I'm at work. I was even getting sad and emotional with my clients' sorrows - I don't usually go that far. You need a sort of tunnel vision at work in order to cope; you need to separate work and home life - this is difficult though. Some of my out-of-work activities are a bit like work - this doesn't help to keep things apart. Also my parenting of my teenage kids gets confused with my handling of teenagers here. John, my husband, will regularly say "Oh, you're using your social work stuff on him!" This is difficult because I don't even vaguely think I'm using my social work!'

'I don't see stress as just concerned with the job. It's part of a number of things going on in one's life. I've been having personal relationship problems, which don't help. Been feeling pretty bad - not sleeping very well. It's been quite worrying as it's the first time this has happened to me. I've been feeling panicky at work - losing my confidence.'

'Separation and loss <u>really</u> gets to me, with me in the middle having to make decisions. It all gets mixed up with my home life as my own children are growing up and leaving me. Also, up to recently my husband's job has put enormous day-to-day stress on him, and therefore me. This makes things very difficult.'

A little over one third of the group highlighted their vulnerability to stress at work when domestic pressures increased: it was hard to share in two emotional worlds, work and family. Furthermore, the mask of professionalism was to be removed when arriving home - it neither felt appropriate nor valid for home problems. But then anxieties flowed more freely onto family members, with sometimes distressing consequences for all involved:

'I seem to take my stress out on the family - it comes in waves. I get so irritated with them - they seem to be the target of my pent up emotions. This really upsets me.'

'Of course the stresses here affect my family. I find I can't talk to them about things - bottle them up. They sense my worry and things get bad.'

Occasionally financial pressures coloured the social worker's life. One participant was frustrated and angry at his financial predicament, and with the lack of support and flexibility shown by his organisation. He described the way insufficient income permeated his relationships and work:

'The block that bugs me now, and my biggest stress, is trying to manage on my income with a family. I've had to carry rather large debts because of my training, and this is causing me more anguish than anything else in the job. It reflects on my performance which makes me very angry. My income is less than my outgoings in ways that I have very little control of at the moment. It gets fairly harrowing at times. Grates with the family so I arrive at work fairly angry at times. It blurs other features of my life and work. When I get home and find my wife's crying, it affects me deeply.'

A picture emerges of social workers with a significantly reduced threshold for experiencing stress at work because of ongoing domestic difficulties, which are in turn aggravated by the emotional residue of a day's work. Under such circumstances virtually any event can precipitate stress.

# 7  Self and coping

A social worker's susceptibility to threat is partly
a matter of personal sensitivities.  Thus how job
features and non-work demands are construed will
depend on an individual's values, attitudes, needs
and expectations in life.  These are some of the
major ingredients of personality, or self, which
slant perceptions and trigger anxieties.  The social
workers provided considerable direct and indirect
material from which to gain a picture of some of the
salient features of self, particularly the more
pervasive characteristics which had some bearing
upon stress.  Most of these were idiosyncratic -
specific individual fears, desires, or prejudices.
In the present chapter I address those features
which, during the data analysis, clustered themati-
cally.  I am now also in a position to examine how
social workers describe the daily business of coping
and surviving - where they succeed, and where they
fail.


IMAGES OF SELF

A frequent claim by the social workers was that they
had a personal drive, or even mission, to help
others help themselves.  The earlier discussion of
dependency and counterdependency suggest that such

statements could sometimes be more characteristic of professional gloss, or rhetoric, than 'true' motives. Certainly, when more deeply reflective of their role and being, this mission statement was often blurred or obscured by different desires or needs. Some talked of their need to have social work to explore or work-through personal problems. Others appeared to be hiding in social work - from troublesome parts of themselves or from the 'unpleasant' world of industry and commerce. Clients and colleagues could provide the major focus for affiliation, and exercising power - which served to further dilute the 'helping others' ethic. The images were variously expressed:

'We all know everyone's in social work because they're screwed up; they don't know what else to do. Somehow they hide their feelings by doing social work. I took the CQSW to feel that I wasn't just useless - I had nothing by my mid twenties. At times I feel more like a client than a social worker - but being more knowledgeable than the average client I can sit back rather than get as aggressive as I feel.'

'It's a need to be needed by people. I've always had the desire to work in helping relationships, although I had a secure middle class background. But it's difficult to be absolutely honest with yourself - I've sometimes thought psychoanalysis would help here.'

'I do it partly for the money - but also for the little bit of power I have. Seeing it all work out and run smoothly satisfies me. But this is so rare now, with the increasing load and the problems piling up. I'd leave if I could get the same money elsewhere.'

'The distressing things in my life sent me into social work - I've had quite a traumatic life. Actually my personal difficulties have helped me to understand and help others. Doing so has helped me.'

Simple altruism is plainly an insufficient explanation for these people's desire to do social work. Their anxiety reactions to what they saw as personal rejection or negation from clients and/or colleagues underlines this conclusion.

It is possible that those who held firmly to the notions of 'a natural reaction to take on people's problems', 'enjoying the challenge in meeting and helping people', 'being in the job because I care about people - they matter', were sheltering under the banner of altruism. It is noteworthy, however, that such individuals - approximately half of the total group - were least tolerant and most threatened by any organisational or administrative apparatus which seemed to deflect attention away from clients and their caring. Their client-centredness seemed genuine and unselfish, in the sense that they were unaware of working to other 'agendas'. Such clarity was redolent in statements of the following sort:

> 'To me it's about people - people matter. Unlike other occupations, we do not deal with "consumers" - it's <u>caring</u> about specific groups and people.'

> 'I'm in this job because I care - care about kids. Sounds a bit trite, but that's where it really is for me.'

> 'I get just about everything out of social work. I got used to the unusual characters around the town where I grew up - and I thought that one day I would like to help people like that. I'm fascinated in others' lives. Enjoy the challenge in meeting people's problems - fitting the answers to the problems. Getting people to <u>relate</u> to me is exceedingly rewarding.'

Philosophical stance

The philosophy of practice of the client-centred social worker reflected humanistic values and pragmatic notions of what would help, or hinder, the well-being of a client. This, as already noted, can be expressed in various forms of 'purity'. However, there was a cluster of eight individuals, comprising all levels of staff, whose personal beliefs and doubts about the meaning of social work left them very ill at ease with their lot. One of the strongest and most loquacious statements of this sort came from a senior social worker:

'I fundamentally doubt the reason for existence of social workers - why spend millions of pounds a year on them? We are being used politically - as first aiders - guides in the concrete jungle. Helping people with complexities which have little to do with them, but are based in wider political issues. Social workers individualise problems - don't see them in the wider context of society, such as patterns of social mobility, housing policy and employment. I suspect my disbelief in doing the job is actually stronger than my commitment - but my style of social work reflects my attempt to live with it. I'm not client centred, but look more to community resources and networks to help. Basically, I'm not at all convinced that the people we see have any greater problems than those we don't see. Most people with seemingly greater problems cope without Social Services. I'm more interested to know why they survive, rather than why they finish up here. Most people arrive here because they are referred by other sources, not because of their own decision.'

Doubts about the efficacy and purpose of social work took some courage to admit as they could threaten a desired sense of purpose. Yet the impression I gained was that once such queries had surfaced there was no turning back - they tended to linger and nag in search of some resolution. Another senior social worker reflects:

'We dabble in people's lives and make enormous assumptions about what we do. We don't sit back and think about what it really means. We can create dependency, undermine the client's worth, and don't move beyond the client into areas which are ultimately probably more important.'

And a team leader thought hard about the social work response to child abuse:

'Here, you've only got to use the words "unexplained bruising" for people to go over the top. There's a lot of kids that get a hell of a hiding that we never hear about - because our channels are so feeble and powers of selection so poor. The injury is often overreacted to - although it certanly worries me that some people are frustrated or provoked to that degree. It's the united professional chorus "that child must come out" that bothers me. So to some degree our philosophies are in conflict with other disciplines. Our outlook on our clients is so totally different from others.'

A sub-theme of the social worker's orientation to their work concerned politicisation. At one level, an all encompassing humanistic, caring approach to clients, a style fostered by some social-work training agencies, can be seen as discordant with the messy and perhaps devious world of organisational politics. My impression was that most main grade social workers viewed politics as generally distasteful, getting in the way of what they saw the job to be about - the client. Their experience informed them of the 'unreasonable' and 'unexplained' blockages and in-fighting, which left them frustrated, powerless and stressed. The more politically active, though, were not automatically rewarded for their effort:

'I get really upset at the lack of motivation amongst social workers to take on wider issues both within and outside the job. Certainly in this organisation any activism just gets a name for yourself. So it saddens me that social workers who are supposed to be intelligent and thinking fail <u>miserably</u> to get themselves together - for professional issues/mutual support. Also there is no enthusiasm from the top to support these needs.'

Senior staff were often more conscious of the political dimenions of their job, and some would express puzzlement or irritation at what they saw as the social worker's naivety in this respect, especially in relation to client welfare. As one team leader remarked:

'I really believe in the sociological and political causes of people's problems. I try

90

to bring some political insight into the
team. Most social workers are probably
apolitical animals. I find it amazing that
some believe social work has nothing to do
with politics! But some people understan-
dably feel, what can they do? But it's all
compromises.'

Control

Losing control over parts of their job was an issue
for one quarter of the group. At the client level,
the desire to retain control over the progress of
affairs was strengthened by the bonds of attachment
from a long working relationship - especially with
children:

'After spending so long working with a kid,
seeing improvements, he goes into a residential institution and changes - regresses. I
lose close contact and see he's unhappy. One
kid gives me most stress. Since he's gone
into the institution, he's lost all his per-
kiness - he's become regimented - "good dis-
cipline". What are we doing to him? I'm
afraid he'll come out at 16 with his character distorted. I'm not at all sure if it's
the right placement for him.'

Others became anxious at the erosion of their
position by certain professionals - such as the
police and medical consultants; and still others had
their own rather particular concerns with respect to
control. For example, the team leader who was
threatened by matrix organisation and changes in his
team because '... my loss of control really gets to
me - I need to objectify things - know where everything is'. The home help organiser who was desperately trying to control a work-flow which depended
upon social workers' actions - with whom she had no
formal influence. And the anxious social worker who
wanted to think more clearly about her decisions,
but was fearful that to do so would mean being
overwhelmed by her clients' demands.

It is noteworthy that much of the concern expressed for control was not an inevitable feature of
the social worker role - it exercised some people
but not others. Yet having a strong personal need
to centre actions upon oneself, to substantially

influence one's work space, or conversely a fear of
losing personal contact, can add a significant
dimension to threat and stress.

Competence

Insofar as the social workers' job provides a major
setting for affirmation, or otherwise, of self competence, it is not surprising to find a number of
people more than aware of their successes and, particularly, their failures. Some of the newer re-
cruits to social work emphasised early difficulties
in feeling or appearing competent:

> 'I was super-conscious of looking competent
> when I first arrived - frightened of admit-
> ting that I couldn't cope. Worst thing you
> can do in a Social Work Department! Safer to
> take it home. But I now realise that we need
> to air things right here - if it's safe
> enough!'

> 'I so need to feel competent with my clients,
> but I just haven't the experience or skills
> yet. I strongly believe in learning by expe-
> rience - yet I considerably lack such expe-
> rience. What can I do?'

Others found their competence challenged when
confronting certain apparently unavoidable sectors
of their work:

> 'When pushed into certain mental health cases
> where I don't feel competent, I get anxious.
> I hate committing people to hospital - for
> example an old lady recently who was just
> rather confused. I didn't want to take the
> GP's judgement - wanted a psychiatrist. But
> there's a risk that she could injure or kill
> herself if I don't recommend commitment to
> hospital.'

> 'With clients I can project an image of com-
> petence - and I believe in this. I should be
> seen as a competent, capable social worker.
> But I find I cannot do this so well with my
> colleagues, especially around organising my-
> self to do the necessary administrative work.
> The anxiety is caused by the effects this has

on other people - I don't want to be seen to
be incompetent.'

'Report writing is probably most critical -
if I don't do it, it will continually nag me.
My own self - my job competence - is tied up
in what the report represents. If I haven't
got it all nicely tied up, then I feel I'm
being inefficient. And if I'm being inefficient, then I'm only being "a SWA".'

The irony of professionally handling problems for
clients which were akin to their own private difficulties was an odd one for some social workers. On
the one hand, they would argue, successfully coming
to terms with their personal life problems could
assist them to help others - they had something
positive to pass on. But, on the other hand, they
felt particularly vulnerable in taking an autho-
ritative stance with clients in areas where they
themselves felt inadequate. The pressures of enacting the role of 'professional', 'competent',
'together' social worker served to reinforce such
inadequacies. One social worker expressed these
feelings with some precision:

'One of my clients dislikes her older kids,
wants me to take them - they're in her way.
I don't like her, probably because she reflects my own difficulties with older kids.
I feel helpless and incapable in this area,
yet I'm the one who's supposed to know everything!'

Fear of failure

Competence feelings overlapped considerably with
fear of failure - the personal disposition to avoid
the pain of failure by side-stepping situations
where some judgement of competence is likely; or
'overperforming', again to protect oneself against
possible censure (eg. Heckhausen, 1967; Birney et
al, 1969). Eleven people described feelings and
situations which indicated a high fear of failure.
Some found the responsibility for taking decisions
about the welfare of clients or staff too onerous
and threatening, so avoided action:

'I sit on the fence. To come off the fence
means I might be wrong, so I prefer someone

else to make the decision. This is a consistent part of me - I don't like to take responsibility for being wrong. It can have disastrous consequences - concerns a person's life.'

'It's all a pretty lose-lose situation for me. If you protect people, and they then get hammered, they're cross with me. If you don't protect them then they get cross with me. It's an impossible position to occupy, so I often just do nothing.'

Others would demonstrate their fear of failure through devoting much energy to gaining approval, or trying to 'plug all the holes' to ensure that nothing would reflect upon them adversely. For example:

'I've always found myself pushed into the position of feeling a failure. I fear authority and always feel I need to _prove_ to my supervisor that I can do my work.'

'Recently it has seemed that whatever I touch has more in it than is on the surface. I have to _give_ all of myself to it. I care about these things a lot. If I don't do everything I can do, I feel I've failed and _I'll_ be particularly to blame if someone gets hurt. I _have_ to avoid this; that's always been me.'

One distinguishing feature of these people was their reluctance, or inability, to admit or enjoy success. Their energy was so defensively deployed that suggestions of success were either denied or deprecated. So when I pointed out what appeared to be a successful client of theirs, or a satisfactory period in their work, they would tell me that it did not feel like that to them - and then proceed to relate the difficulties they had at those times. Similarly, praise from their supervisor was discredited as false, or undeserved.


COPING

The social workers described, or implied, characteristic ways of responding to threat and stress.

94

Some would only recognise stress difficulties through their attempts to cope; in other words, what they were <u>doing</u> differently alerted them to the stress problem (see Table 4.1).

The dominant style of coping was an internalisation of difficulties; a 'bottling-up' or compartmentalisation of anxiety in the hope that it would disappear spontaneously, or could be released elsewhere. Some talked of this as a deliberate, conscious strategy; others assumed it was unconscious - 'It sort of happens automatically'. Rarely, though, was such emotional self-protection foolproof. For example:

'You can't offload your problems and stress onto a client, so you internalise it - bring it back to the office. I try to talk to someone - just get someone to <u>listen</u>, that's all you need! When things get really tough, though, I cope by escapism - plan a future in other work, back to university, or whatever. Try to kid myself the present hell can't last for ever. Doesn't always work, though.'

'I don't go around getting angry or crying about my stress - I sort of bury it. When I feel hurt and angry I put up barriers - but it's not a conscious process. There are few who I can trust here sufficiently to talk about how I feel. But this confuses people who know I've got problems - they don't know how to talk to me - they back off.'

'I don't let my anger out at work - not "professional". Swimming helps - I can forget everything in the water; but I don't do it regularly. I eat too much. I can see it but I can't do anything about it. I don't even take time off when I'm sick - I feel it would push too much on my colleagues. It's a frenetic life style, without time to really <u>listen</u> to clients. The job has lost its attraction - I just try to cover myself. We often think "My God, how can we carry on?".'

'Problems are often gone after I've cooked a meal in the evening - but they might come back. I'll be in bed churning things over. I'm practically an insomniac at times - it's the pressure of work and anything else. But the journey in the car to and from work seems to provide the necessary transition from winding up or winding down. It provides the necessary psychological distance.'

. Such privatisation of anxiety, encapsulating it, appeared one response to a job which could be relentless in its emotional demands, but at the same time required a 'stable' persona - for clients and, often, for colleagues. Added to this, some did not wish to burden their own families with their work worries, but were equally concerned to avoid shouldering the domestic angst. As more avenues for tension-dissipation were blocked, or shut off, the more devious became the channels of anxiety expression:

'After 12 months in the job I stopped taking the job home. I now realise that I can't be God so I don't take problems home. I can now forget about things at home - except at night. When you've gone to bed it's difficult to block off the problems and stresses. The whirls go on, especially after the build up of pressures.'

'One of the unusual things about this job is you can be talking to people about their problems from 9 to 5 without a break, but to go home to the same position is impossible. So I just want to switch off from family problems. I feel so guilty with the children about this.'

'I don't hold stress over time - such as with headaches. I can push it quite deep down - diversionary tactics - fiddling with the central heating system - displacement. Sometimes stressful things vanish without trace and then pop up without warning.'

Some people could internalise their anxieties and later re-work them, or re-construe them, until they were disarmed, safe. Again this could be a private process which sometimes took place during a relaxing activity - such as meditation, sport or a 'do it yourself' hobby. The style of one senior social worker exemplifies this approach:

'I seem to have adapted over the years. I used to feel far more vulnerable earlier on in social work - less well coping - felt very stressed. Far more sleepless nights five years ago than now. I regard life as problematic for everyone. I have as many problems as my clients. The way you define things determines your response to them. I get a lot of personal satisfaction from leisure mechanical activities. <u>Essential</u> contrast to my job; deep pleasure, tangible - A <u>will</u> lead to B.'

A team leader offers a similar viewpoint:

'When I'm stressed I cope by internalising it to get through the day. Then I'll go home and <u>do</u> things physically while mulling it over. I don't chat to my wife - she's got enough on her plate. I sort it out that way.'

A mental reconstruction of problems leading to a reduction in threat, or intimidation, is a form of confrontation which can successfully build upon initial internalisation. More overt confrontation was a rare occurrence in this group. Only three talked of 'fighting' their way out of difficulties, or persistently looking for new directions of solution. Far more typical were flight responses - avoiding, denying, psychologically and/or physically withdrawing. All reactions which normally assist in protecting the individual from excessive pain or anxiety - for a time, at least:

'I avoid the difficulties - back off. Rationalise them. But it doesn't go away - problem hangs around, reappears, haunts me.'

'I can't keep adding hours - I've seen what this has done to others. I avoid the painful areas; I'm constantly making excuses for my lack of action.'

'I've been waking up at nights tossing and turning - thinking about clients. I'm not paid to worry about them when I'm out of work - this worries me. One indicator, that I hate admitting to, is sometimes I've had enough. Just switch off and go home. Feel

cheesed off with everything - people I'm to
see, transfer slips, paper work. It's <u>not</u>
visit a client until the last minute, or <u>even</u>
not at all. It's a real low spot. I just
quit.'

'I've been having a very bad time, so much so
that I've run out of empathy for others. I
can't see others' points of view any more. I
just want to get out - walk out of the web of
social services. I get so exhausted defen-
ding my integrity, which has been questioned.
I'm absolutely spaced out at night, and <u>so</u>
tense. I can't win.'

'When I get home the here-and-now things
still buzz through my mind - very difficult
indeed to cut off. I need 3-4 days on holiday to forget about things before I can
relax. It's horrible coming back. When I
get overwhelmed, which does happen, I just
have to withdraw - leave the office complete-
ly. I can get desperate for a rest, as it's
impossible to cut off in the office. But
when this happens it spells failure to me.
Things still have to be done when I get back
- it's <u>my</u> responsibility to chase clients. I
end up taking short cuts - especially with
the paperwork.'

The most comfortable copers were those who
referred to their 'survival kit'; an expression
evoking images of a variety of aids available to
suit the particular problem. It was a term employed, usually, by more experienced staff in describing the political manoeuvrings, types of
confrontation, psychological defences and forms of
relaxation they had learnt to adopt in order to
manage the complexities of their life, and survive
without excessive personal cost. For example:

'The longer I'm in social work the more I've
found it terribly important to develop a
personal survival kit - something you've got
to work out yourself. The anxiety feelings
are not as bad now as they used to be - but I
can switch off now, especially at weekends.
I also cope by throwing myself into the work.
Quite stupid, really, as I work far too many
hours. But I survive now - by not revealing

too much to my supervisor as I'll be handed
out more work; by lowering my standards -
prevents the system making me a nervous
wreck!'

'I've learned from the bad times. I haven't
grown less caring or compassionate, but I've
begun to realise what I can do or can't do -
that I'm not God. Learned that some things
I've got absolutely no control over. Doesn't
stop me fighting consultants at hospital, but
when they say "no", I don't blame myself any
more. The problem is still there, but it's
not a hurtful problem.'

Such contingent styles were unusual, however.
Most people had yet to acquire such agility, being
more locked into a single, and often defensive, form
of coping - and illness played its part here. As
earlier-mentioned, 'going sick' was a recognised
form of stress avoidance or recuperation. As such
it provided a good escape route for those who wished
to use it, or exploit it. Once defined as 'ill', by
self and others, it was excusable not to re-confront
one's threats.

The need and adequacy of others' support in coping
with stress was regularly mentioned. It emerged as
a complex issue, and is one I address in detail in
the next chapter.

# 8 Support

In one of our meetings a social worker spoke with poignancy about her difficulties in coping with the demands of a particular client when added to her home pressures. I asked if she had shared her concerns with any colleagues. 'Oh no!' she retorted 'I wouldn't want to be social worked by them.' She then recoiled with a look of horror on her face, 'God, what am I saying? I can use my social work skills on clients but I can't accept them for myself?'

This kind of double standard was expressed in a variety of ways. It was an odd feeling for those (a little over half the group) who found themselves facing, and contributing to, a wall of interpersonal evasiveness or even indifference inside the office, while professing just the opposite to clients ouside of the office. They were puzzled and agitated. It raised uncomfortable questions about their profes- sional competence - surely their skills were rele- vant on their own doorstep? They also felt helpless victims of a climate which provided little of the emotional support they so desired, and which could aggravate pre-existing tensions.

A senior social worker summarised the position as follows:

'This is a particularly caring group of
people, but they play a charade with each
other's problems and stresses. There's a
sort of collusive arrangement not to talk to
people about their stresses. If it's linked
to a home situation there's a shame that
they, as social-workers, feel stressed. They
feel guilty that they can't resolve it. No
one stops to ask why this should be the case.
One social worker has a handicapped sister
who's incredibly demanding; and another's
recently lost her husband. And people say
"How are you? Fine? Where are you going
for your holiday?" It's ridiculous.'

Few who observed such aspects of their professional life were at ease with the paradox it
presented. They felt that things ought to be different, but were generally at a loss to know how to
make them so. The climate was too pervasive to
influence. The locus of the difficulty was variously described. It included personal intolerance, the
illegitimacy of seeking support from colleagues ('a
social worker should not be seen as a client'),
closely guarded professional activity, and the
administrative features of an organisation which
evolves quite distinctly from the professional
values of its practitioner members. Some of the
social workers' own words elucidate these points:

'Oddly, I can make allowances for clients
which I don't for colleagues. Generally I'm
glad to listen to moans and groans of
clients, but not of colleagues. For example,
helping a colleague through a crisis she's
now having puts an added stress on the whole
team. I then get cross with her because
she's ill, and she can't help it. That's an
inadequacy in me - lack of tolerance.'

'We're not caring of each other - maybe we
expect more of our colleagues than we've got
to give. Some social workers really do care,
but some are rarely in the office, don't
communicate much, and when they do have a
problem they don't get much support from the
office. A comfortable office should help us
share the good and bad things. If you only
share the bad things, people go off you.
We're often too mean to share the good.'

'I've always thought that the Social Services
are a helping agency - but its ability to
help staff is not as good as one might expect
from the outside. It takes on "agency" features rather than social work principles.'

'I used to feel sharing was a good thing when
I worked in a hospital team - it was seen as
good to have several viewpoints; provided a
rounder view of what's going on. But somehow
this is felt to be "bad" in Social Services -
equated with "not nice", "uncomfortable".
And the client can pick up your frustration,
which can't be too good.'

The dualistic feature of whom one supports challenged those who espoused democracy in social work
practice. For some it led to the unsettling realisation that a structural power relationship with a
client was perhaps a more important part of their
professional control than they had thought, an
arrangement which of course was less tenable with
fellow peers. So one could not 'social work' peers
nor would one wish to be social worked, subordi-
nated, by them. Additionally, as suggested in
Chapter 5, many had doubts about the value and
efficacy of social work practice, concerns which
could be camouflaged within the client relationship:
but not so with peers who were ostensibly as wise as
oneself - too wise for comfort. Those who thought
in this manner frequently invalidated any useful
support that a colleague might provide as a person
beyond his or her professional role. The social
work relationship ruled the interaction.

The position with senior staff was more complicated. To be 'social worked' by one's supervisor
meant accepting that something was wrong with oneself, a pathological role-state, in front of someone
who had the power, and to some extent the obligation, to make judgements about one's professional
competence and worth in the organisation. This
added to some people's unease about revealing certain personal stress problems to their supervisors.

Beyond the supervisory relationship, a number of
different avenues for professional and/or general
emotional support were located. Home and other
extra-mural relationships could be important, as
well as religious faith:

'I can talk about a lot of things with my wife; she's a social worker and has similar feelings. We make time to help each other. I also have time with a colleague at another agency. I trained with her, and I work through a lot with her. She's a sympathetic person at a deeper level. Inside the office, though, I've been disappointed. Some of us can't bear to do things with "equals" that we can do to clients. Our inability to relate to each other in this way might signal the extent we are unable to work with clients.'

'I'm lucky in having a very stable husband. He does understand me. I can go home to him with all my stresses and unload it on him. The dear man just switches his deaf aid off and just listens - grunting in the right places and saying the right things. I'm also bolstered by my Christian beliefs.'

'My religious activities provide the community support which is so important to me. My "natural" support is through my boss, but there's so much politicking between us that it causes me far more stress than stress alleviation.'

Whether or not 'the boss' provided the desired support was partly a matter of the history and quality of personal relationship between the two parties. In principle the supervisor's position legitimised a form of support that could be unacceptable between peers. The unbalanced relationship set out expectations of supporter and supportee. In theory the supervisor - senior social worker or team leader - had the experience, wisdom and proper function to prop and sustain whenever necessary, a role that some workers could come to depend on (see also the section on supervision in Chapter 5):

'I tell bits to the team - but not very much. My team leader is critical - I need to talk out my problems with her. I became paralysed when she was away sick. I can't share these things with other team members. Talking to one person doesn't necessarily remove the problem, but it does often provide a line of action and reduce conflicts. I talk a lot to my husband in this way.'

'I'm OK in the office as long as I have an anchor to return to - such as the team leader; someone I can relate to. If I know that person's there, I'll overcome the stresses this department puts on me.'

'I talk things out with Mike, our team leader. I'd rather go to him than my immediate supervisor. I also have a very good relationship with one particular colleague - but the team has shifted in composition so many times, so this is pretty precarious. But I can get more depressed if there's somebody with me than when I'm alone. I don't stop being depressed by talking about it. Talking can increase the intensity and importance of it, making things worse. I'm an isolated person who does need to talk, but on my terms.'

Sometimes, as illustrated above, someone would bypass their main supervisor in search of more adequate support at a higher level in the office organisation, or elsewhere in the wider organisation. Yet with such heavy reliance on a specific supervisor, or surrogate supervisor, it is perhaps not surprising that expectations of desired support were not always met, and sometimes points of sustained security or help could not be found inside or outside of the organisation. At least a third of the total group felt this way. They presented a picture of isolation and loneliness:

'I have to manage alone - my supervisor and team leader are away, or have more than sufficient problems of their own, to be able to assist me. I do need help with the deeper issues within me - but I will have to go elsewhere for this.'

'I had a friend who was also a peer "supervisor", but he's left. There's no-one else I trust.'

'Although I do talk to my colleagues about a few of my anxieties, it is ultimately my problem and responsibility. I have to learn to live with it. Sometimes, though, I get angry that I don't get the type of support that helps me sort out work difficulties

where I feel inexperienced - out of my
depth.'

'I stew on it at home. I've no-one at home
to talk to. My supervisor says that my job
suffers because of this. My husband can't
get a job down here so I only see him at
weekends. This does affect me badly. At
home I am now just like a vegetable, stewing
away.'

These people were main grade social workers.
Senior staff had their own difficulties. As
'absorbers of others' stresses', they would con-
sciously attempt to protect staff from undue anxieties and avoid burdening them with their own
personal problems (but not very effectively according to some social workers). An attitude of protection was taken towards supervisory colleagues as
well - 'They've got enough on their plates without
my problems' was a typical statement. Through this
some felt increasingly isolated; and when the few
available channels with top level staff became
fogged with political tension the supervisor could
find himself, or herself, very much alone. One team
leader describes this phenomenon:

'My main source of support, now things are so
bad for me, should be my boss - the Area
Director. But as some of my anger and resentment is directed towards him, he's not
the best person to hear me. It would place
him in an impossible position. So where am I
to go? I feel isolated, lonely.'

Personal struggles from a perceived lack of support could be found in all five of the teams
studied. Yet the spread of dissatisfaction was
uneven, varying from one team where considerable
peer and supervisory support was evident at both
professional and general emotional levels (actually
a somewhat arbitrary and unreal distinction for many
social workers), to teams where little coherent
patterns of support were detectable.

The majority of Team B eulogised about the support
available. Typical statements were:

'I feel it's a very good team here -
everyone's very supportive - can see when

105

someone's under organisational pressure.
People do this with me. For example, if I'm
staying after 1.00pm, they tell me to leave.
I'd go to whoever's around for support. Our
team leader is included but he's not quite as
"in" as everyone else.'

'I do talk about worries in the team - we all
do in this team. But I think this is excep-
tional. When I visit other teams it doesn't
feel the same. For example, in one team
there are some people with personal problems
who wouldn't be allowed to hold on to them
here. We'd share them. You can be honest
here and people accept you for this.'

'I feel I've come into a good team - a lot of
support. I think I'd have had more stress if
that hadn't been the case. I've always had
someone to turn to to seek advice.'

Few of the suspicions of 'social working' one
another were evident amongst this group. Many
people talked of being able to 'be yourself here',
implying a way relaxing out of role and accepting
each other as fallible individuals. Such mutual
trust found links with the team leader's activities
in promoting support. Indeed his integrative
meetings with staff on professional matters - which
he took most seriously and sensitively judging from
his and others' reports - were probably critical
ingredients in helping to set the supportive
climate. It would seem that a regular mutual
sharing of work-related issues, if managed construc-
tively, can sow the seeds for a more open support
network. This did not mean that certain social
workers would not take their own routes to support,
or react against the team leader's efforts. But
even they talked of a basically comfortable atmosphere in the team and a freedom to move in a number
of different directions.

Where there was less cohesion around a team leader
- which was the case in all teams but the aforementioned - support was more fragmented and idiosyncratic. Main grade social workers saw some seniors
as more supportive than others. 'Supportiveness'
meant different things to different people. It
included qualities or behaviours such as availa-
bility, decisiveness and empathy, acting as a

political buffer, being a listener, adviser and expert, and providing a shoulder to cry on. Novices to social work looked for rather more prescribed expert advice and guidance in field and organisational matters than did experienced social workers. Whether or not a senior 'fitted' with the expectations of a supervisee and vice versa was more often a result of chance and mutual negotiation than of design. When the supervisory relationship became strained, both parties could find strategies of easing apart. For example, the supervisor may become 'unavoidably unavailable' and the supervisee may go through the motions of being supervised but in fact reveal and heed little.

A select number of peers comprised the most common support, peers from within a particular faction or expertise in an office or, occasionally, from somewhere in the wider organisation. At times a worker felt it necessary to locate a professional soul-mate in another social services setting - perhaps because of an unusual specialism. Moving beyond the office and its politics for support was seen as a positive advantage by some as it provided an important psychological distance through which communication could flourish in ways which seemed impossible when close to the job and colleagues.

Patterns of peer support took a while to form and mature. Sometimes personal and professional crises were significant events in their shaping. Those new to social work and to the organisation did not have the benefit of such an informal network and were potentially most vulnerable and unprotected should their formal supervisor be unable to meet their needs. Indeed, part of the business of survival in social work was described as battling through this initiation and finding one's own form of support. Some senior staff went as far as claiming that this process was what the work was all about - the raison d'etre of the job:

'Professional colleague support is about the only thing that makes the stresses of this job bearable. Support comes from being with certain people who are of similar status and standing - senior colleagues with specialist functions. The "team" is an artificial entity, but there are close contacts between individuals. Indeed, it's the fact that

other social workers in our region relate to
me when <u>they're</u> under stress, that makes my
job worthwhile.  For me, there's limited
satisfaction out of the client end of the
job.'

# Endpiece

This part of the book has portrayed details, many of them intimate, of a group of 40 social workers. Their articulateness was in part a reflection of their stress state - a desire to talk and unburden themselves of some of their anxieties. It was, it seems, something they were rarely able to do.

The facets of stress highlighted in Figure 3.1 remain a modest approximation of the complexity of the social workers' experiences - yet they are a reasonable guide. Within them I find a picture of social workers devoting a great deal of their energy towards organising themselves to survive the day. There is the impression of considerable groping and blundering in acquiring sufficient professional skills to 'get by'. With clients, the ambiguities are often greater than the certainties, resulting in much unrewarded personal effort. Many social workers were clearly client-centred - an orientation which nevertheless disguised a range of different personal motives and sensitivities. Some clients were used to prop up the social worker's ailing self image, while others reminded the worker of his or her own fragilities and problems.

The outward flow of energy towards clients was easily interrupted or blocked. Bureaucratic demands, paperwork, other professionals and home pressures were generally received as unwelcome intruders to be worked against, rather than worked for or with. They were not 'part of the job'. This created a certain defensive approach towards work, which was hardened by what I can best describe as a fearful atmosphere. Even within the more relaxed teams there was, not far below the surface, an uneasiness and apprehension about statutory respon- sibilities - that they may not respond with suffi- cient speed or adequacy to prevent a child being abused or an old person dying from neglect.

Chronic problems from thwarted effort and anxious vigilance are hard to manage, and causes are attri- buted in all directions - to self, to supervisor, to management, to the 'nature of social work'. As no permanent solutions emerge, stress, to varying degrees, becomes part of the job - often a weary and wearing part, but an accepted part. But if dis- abling stress is to be avoided and the social worker is to remain a survivor in the job, emotional sup- port is crucial. Here arrangements span from the ad hoc to the planned, the former predominating. Sup- port can thrive within peer groups - but many are still left feeling naked and lonely, without ade- quate lifelines.

# Part III
# Inside counselling

# Introductory points

The research material that I have presented has resulted from my counselling activities. But the counselling was more than a vehicle for the research data: it was aimed at providing tangible assistance for those with stress problems. I have outlined the counselling rationale in Part I. This part of the book indicates how this rationale worked in practice - the kinds of things I did and what I attempted to achieve.

What follows are selective illustrations of the mood and characteristics of Phases II to IV of the counselling, pictures which emphasise my own role in shaping events and outcomes. Hopefully this will help to de-mystify the activity of counselling which is often portrayed as an intuitive process, depending upon the 'chemistry' of the situation and the 'gut feelings' of the counsellor.

This does not mean that I am able to offer neat explanations for everything that went on. What I am able to say, however, is that the development of the counselling, and the nature of many of my interventions, were matters of conscious control and the deliberate exercise of certain skills within a particular framework of action and help.

# 9 Exploring perspectives and problems

Phase I of the counselling had set the groundwork for the counselling relationship. I had provided the social workers with information on who I was, what I was doing, and what benefits might accrue from their participation. Public discussions had taken place where, to some extent, individual concerns could be addressed. Phase II meetings, the subject of this chapter, brought me into private contact with those who wished to use me: a potentially more threatening situation for them as it was their first serious gesture to me that they may be in need of help.

My initial objective in this phase was to establish rapport in a way that would make the social worker feel sufficiently comfortable to begin to talk about himself, or herself. I would re-introduce myself, talk about what I had been doing so far in the social worker's office, and outline the way things between us could progress - the counselling phases and stress framework. I talked of the confidentiality of our sessions, and the way I was using my tape recordings. I indicated that my aim was to respond to any of their stress issues in as practical a way as possible.

I did not want to over individualise and 'proble-matise' the atmosphere at this early stage, so I emphasised my interest in hearing generally about their views on stress in their office and in social work. When I received signs - pauses, anticipatory glances, no more questions - that the social worker felt ready to move on, I put the general question, 'What, if anything, does stress mean to you in your work?' - my first attempt to help them explore their stresses. Normally I would receive a fast and suc-cinct reply. For example:

'I can't envisage a life without stress. I'm sure I'm one of those characters who go round looking for stress even when it's not there.'

'Stress varies. Depends on what the work is. It's often other people's stress which ref-lects on me.'

'It's all about the management of feelings. It happened to me this morning. The stress of having to suppress feelings because they're not strictly relevant to the task in hand.'

I regarded such early statements as important. They represented some thing or area that the social worker felt able to address with me - so I would encourage elaboration, verbally and non-verbally. Frequently my signs of affirmation and individual attention were sufficient to trigger an outpouring of views and feelings: worries, prejudices, fears and opinions. They appeared as a spontaneous release of tension. I would listen carefully for recurrent themes and particularly difficult prob-lems. Sometimes a person would stop or hesitate in 'full flow', looking a little embarrassed:

'Gosh, what am I saying? This must sound such a muddle!'

'I haven't talked to anyone like this - doesn't make any sense.'

I would try to reassure them that I did want to hear what they had to say, in what ever form it was expressed. One social worker stopped and offered a more analytic reflection of what he was experien-cing:

'It's interesting. My recollections from a counselling workshop are that it isn't the quality or skill of attention that the client responds to - it's the fact that they are getting attention. Even now, we grossly underestimate this in social work.'

In this manner, several people indicated their curiosity with the counselling process, and began to examine their own client work. They also made connections between my work and theirs - a perceived link which intrigued them, and also enhanced my credibility in their eyes.


EMPATHIC FEEDBACK

I continued to coach the discussion and self-exploration in two ways. The first was through empathic feedback. My restating, rephrasing, or gentle questioning of what I felt they were feeling or expressing. My intention was to encourage deeper reflection on a particular problem or point to clarify its nature and details. For example:

Social Worker: 'When things are going wrong for the kids I'm working with I suppose I feel as upset as they do. Well, not as upset as them. I can't as it's not happening to me.'

Me: 'You seem to be saying that you get emotionally involved, but only up to a point.'

Social Worker: 'Yes. Some separation is crucial. I feel very sorry for social workers who become desperate for help because they become too intimate with their clients. There are cases I get more involved with than others. There's one, Mary, .....'

--------

Team Leader: 'I believe in the worth of the individual. Social workers are so often held down - I try to help them grow and develop.'

Me: 'I can see that you have a strong concern for individuals, for people. How do you think this comes over to your staff?'

116

Team Leader:  'Well ... er ... it varies.  I have enormous difficulties with one person who has told me I am very paternalistic.  I internalise remarks like that.  I've gone through a year of stress with this person.  I go home and worry.  I don't worry about clients - but I do about staff.  It is a paternalistic thing, I think.'

Not infrequently I would struggle to achieve the social workers' perspectives.  Sometimes because of my ignorance of their professional terms and jargon, but more often because the fragments of information I was hearing were too small or disconnected for me to get a fair sense of their frameworks or meanings.  To increase the information base I would ask for re-explanations, to the extent that the social workers indicated that I was understanding them correctly.  I considered it my role to receive their perceptions as fully and 'accurately' as possible, but to respect their own positons by not evaluating what I had heard.  My evaluation might be appropriate in helping them to manage stress; but this would come later in the counselling process.  Nevertheless I viewed the very process of empathic feedback, with its clarification activities, as a crucial first step in helping the social worker to appraise his or her problems.


CONCRETE ACCOUNTS

The second way of proceeding was by encouraging specific examples and illustrations of what was being said.  This overlapped with empathic feedback, but aimed more at clarifying specific stress areas - such as signs of stress, personal vulnerabilities and coping styles.  So, for example, general statements about stress could be 'sharpened-up' as follows:

Social Worker:  'Of course, stress is around with me all the time in this job.'

Me:  'What happens to you - your feelings.'

Social Worker:  'Ah.  I get very tired and tense in client interviews.  I can't think clearly.  Sometimes I'll get splitting headaches as well.'

Me:  'Can you tell me about the last client interview when you felt like this?'

My task here was to edge the social worker beyond vague generalities towards the specifics and essence of his or her experiences. These would form the substance of self reflection and the stress analysis to come.  I would encourage as much descriptive detail about circumstances associated with stress - other people, relationships, particular settings, beyond-work experiences, historical/biographical influences, and so on.  I would ask questions of the sort:  'When did that last happen?'  'What was going on at the time?'  'Tell me what led up to those feelings'.  Frequently, terse initial statements could develop into rich and revealing stories, when handled in this way.  For example:

Me:  'When do those stress symptoms flare up?'

Team Leader:  'Frequently!'

Me:  'Could you tell me about the most recent occasion?'

Team Leader:  'Two days ago with my own boss, who causes me the most stress of all.'

Me:  'What happened?'

Team Leader:  'I had been involved in a two-day intense discussion with a group of managers, where we came out with our own priorities for the new organisation.  My boss then sent a memo to Headquarters containing his own views, but none of ours!  I was angry because my investment has always been to get the management group functioning in a way to get its voice felt.  I was angry because it wasn't bloody fair that one of the most important memos went forward with just <u>one</u> person's point of view on it.  I feel conned, misrepresented.  It maddens me.  I don't really know why it gets to me like that. Rivalry?  Wanting to be the boss?  It might be worth exploring this.  These incidents leave me with enormous stress feelings.'

Inside this recollection are all manner of hints about personal vulnerabilities, styles of interaction and sources of threat which I would later piece together, along with the implications from his other statements and stories. Consistent worries across different perceived situations could indicate dominating concerns, perhaps rooted deeply in the personality - concerns, for example, for security, achievement, or self worth. Other difficulties or stresses may be more situationally contained, or episodic - such as when the social worker visits certain clients or attends particular meetings.

Sometimes a social worker's inability to back-up or illustrate a contention could be just as revealing, suggesting less obvious parts of personality, or a manner of self-presentation - as illustrated by this extract:

Social Worker: 'I so often have to go to my supervisor, and tell him how bloody <u>awful</u> things are for me.'

Me: 'It sounds as though you feel very stressed when you see him ....'

Social Worker: 'I am!'

Me: 'What kinds of things make you feel so awful?'

Social Worker: 'Well, I <u>say</u> that to him, but I suppose I don't really mean it. What I'm asking for is a pat on the head telling me I'm not really so bad at things after all.'

It is likely that concrete accounts and recollections, such as those above, provide a relatively comfortable vehicle for people's selective perceptions. How close they are to what 'really' happened is less material than them being a valid indicator of the sense that is being made of the events there and then - the phenomenological context to problems and threats. It is within such personal definitions of situations that specific assumptions about self and others may be found.

Choosing when I should engage in empathic feedback or seek specific examples of an issue or problem was guided by the apparent stress content or stress relevance of what was being said. Sometimes this

was obvious to me from the clear stress overtones -
'That was the worst period of my life'; 'I was sick
for six weeks when that crisis happened'; 'I felt
utterly depressed and inadequate working with that
client'. But just as often the undertones of stress
caught my attention; statements implying anxiety,
threat, insecurity, vulnerabilities. The following
were typical of these:

'I'm lucky that my supervisor can take the
pressure I put on him - but he's been questioning this lately which makes me rather
unsettled.'

'When I see kids having gone through residential establishments, I quite frankly feel we
haven't done too much for them. So am I
going to put another kid through that?'

'You know, one of our tasks is preventing
people coming into care. This needs a fair
amount of input in many situations. Needs
time allocation. Especially teenage kids who
are presented to me by police, parents,
schools, as beyond parental control. What
can I do?'

'I try not to worry about the load - try to
do what I can and no more. But there is a
need to account for my time to explain to
people why I'm doing what I'm supposed to be
doing.'

COPING

How social workers coped with their stress problems
- their struggles, failures and successes - was
normally part of, interwoven with, the accounts of
their circumstances. But when this was not the
case, I would ask direct questions, such as:

'What do you do when all that pressure hits
you?'

'I can sense how overbearing those situations
must be. How do you manage?'

'You say you bottle it all up. What happens
when you get home?'

120

'If that is your main source of stress, in what ways do you tackle it?'

Typical replies were:

'I took it to my team leader - but never again! He had no real sense of my problem. I felt humiliated.'

'I get home quite desperate for someone to talk to, but I'm alone. I can cry - it depresses me so.'

'I eat and eat, tear about, smoke. It's awful. Nothing seems to go right.'

'I ring Headquarters and get no reply. I leave messages; no-one phones back. All the time my client is in a critical position. It feels like a dead end to me, like hitting my head against a brick wall.'

'Well, every time I begin to get the paper-work straight, along comes another emergency. I've pleaded with my team leader to re-allocate work, but he seems helpless.'

These all provided leads, or clues, towards appropriate help; where support might be required, where new strategies of confrontation could be discussed, where personal skills could be improved, where anxiety management could be important. They would contribute to the more focussed stress analysis in Phase III of the counselling - the subject of the next chapter.

# 10  Clarifying stress problems: preparing for action

The breadth of Phase II was complemented by the sharper focus of Phase III. I moved the counselling towards sorting and sifting perceptions into actionable stress problems, and planning any necessary action.

When I had the opportunity of more than one meeting with a social worker I would prepare a summary stress analysis for feedback at the beginning of the second meeting. This was based upon my notes and the tape recording, and was designed to deliberately move the social worker's attention towards stress problems that I saw as amenable to possible action. They were my re-statements, or re-ordering, of their words, and they represented the first clear 'sense-making' activity of all that they had told me. I regarded the analysis as a tentative one, to be subject to their own modifications and corrections. It was a device intended to <u>enable</u> the social workers in their actions, and not to be received as an immutable God-like utterance from myself. I explained this to them, and presented the analysis together with my particular uncertainties, doubts and gaps in information. I can best convey the process through some examples, using my actual stress-analysis summary notes.

# STRESS ANALYSIS: JOHN

**Major stress problem** Competence with clients

**Context** Invested much of skill in training for deaf clients.
Seeks a new occupational identity.
Came out of training with a very important ingredient missing - the social work side of deafness.
Limited skills in 'signing'.
Strong belief in learning by experience, yet considerably lacks such experience.
High self-standards to be a good social worker.
High standards not met - threatens need to be competent and self image.

**Coping** Early avoidance, but now confronting.
Keeps trying to achieve a dialogue with clients, but rarely seems to manage this.
Strong experience of failure.
Further belief that clients will suffer - adds to failure.

**Consequences** Stress. Having to cope with problems and failures.
Burns up much of available energy.
Little spare capacity to deal with administration - an added burden (but not the burden).

**Action possibilities** Re-examine job demands.
Are self-expectations realistic? Too much too soon?
Try less difficult clients first. Could case allocation be influenced?
Schedule more meetings with professional colleagues outside of the Department.
Negotiate with Team Leader and Area Director for time off to increase signing skills.

John listened attentively while I talked around the above points, shared my impressions with him, and floated ideas for action. His first comments both reinforced and qualified the analysis:

'I don't feel competent. Emotionally I'm failing, but intellectually I don't expect to be competent; it takes three years. I've got that time to get somewhere. I'm still getting something out of the job - it's not all minus. But I am glad that it came over that the client is most important, because I was wondering whether I was avoiding looking at that by using the administrative problems.'

He gradually talked more and more of his need for extra support and we explored ways in which this could be obtained. We progressed through a number of 'exploration-challenge-resolution' cycles where the viability of possible ways foward were quizzed and challenged by me, to result in John's tentative acceptance or rejection of a particular route to support. In this way potentially supportive individuals were listed from inside and outside the organisation, societies and groups which represented his interests were identified, and different ways of cultivating new contacts were reviewed. These gradually cohered into John's action intentions:

'I must now make space and time for this support and not get overloaded with other stuff. It's a problem I can now clearly recognise so I will set to work creating a support group for myself - no-one's going to do it for me!'

Generally, my higher profile was typical of Phase III interventions. As in the above example, social workers would usually use my summary images of them to think about themselves and to review their problems. I would always encourage what they viewed as feasible action, although I would press them to clarify the details of their intentions until I was satisfied that they had a reasonable chance of achieving them. This, I hoped, would leave the social worker with rather more than just a 'good feeling' that something could be done. So, in John's case, I concluded our meeting only when I heard some definite statement as to how he would go about creating his support group.


STRESS ANALYSIS: DIANA

Major stress problem   Working relationship with
    partner, Alan.

**Context** Needs to 'do something with Alan to get anywhere in the job'.
She's an 'ideas person', 'nit picker', not a 'setter-up' like Alan.
They are different people. She annoys Alan by not cooperating and communicating with him. She feels she unsettles and stresses him.
They are a good counterweight to each other, but they cannot cooperate well in some tasks. 'Are we the wrong people for each other?'

**Threat** Problem concerns a core, specific part of the job which stops her committing herself to things.
Directly relates to feelings of adequacy and inadequacy.

**Coping** She backs off. Too threatening and close to tackle or disturb.
Rationalises it out in terms of macro/structural problems.
Inaction and avoidance.

**Consequences** Problem lingers and nags, but remains unsolved.
Stressful.

**Action possibilities** Diana and Alan re-examine their roles.
Can Diana find a more satisfying role with Alan by confronting the problem with him? My support for them?

Diana looked tense and a little uncomfortable as I fed back my impressions to her; I was touching upon a sensitive and difficult situation:

'I've made mistakes in the past - inventing problems between me and someone else. I'm in a dilemma knowing whether or not Alan has a problem. But there _is_ a problem for _me_.'

I asked her if, on balance, she would still prefer to leave things as they are. She responded:

'But that would be like dashing to the end of a springboard - then walking back again.'

I explored her avoidance behaviour within the context of other avoidance patterns she had revealed. She was wrestling with her conscience and self interest:

'My natural reaction is to withdraw - to protect myself. Very desirable at times. But if I'm encouraged not to run away, I don't. I guess I've got to tackle the problem, otherwise I'm running round and getting nowhere.'

I encouraged her not to run away this time, and offered a helping hand. I suggested that we should be prepared to find that she alone was the one with the 'presenting' problem, but that did not mean that Alan could not have a role in helping to improve matters. She gradually became more enthusiastic about seeing Alan - if I would make the arrangements. I did this, and Alan agreed that we should all meet. (Some of the outcomes of this are discussed in the next chapter.)

My role with Diana moved beyond just encouraging her own action - it involved my direct and continuing support. Without this she would have probably felt far too anxious to move forward.


STRESS ANALYSIS: ELEANOR

Major stress problem  Lack of clerical back-up.

Context  No help in preparing papers, typing, filing. Leads to feeling of overload, pressure and muddle in work.

Threat  Unable to be adequately prepared for important meetings - reflects on her importance, which hurts.
Threatens role identity, 'Am I a highly paid clerk?'
Personality issue - needs to influence and control.

Coping  'Tried everything, but failed - formal and informal channels.'
'Unable to locate source of power.'

<u>Consequences</u>   Exhausted and frustrated.  Tense
and anxious.
Problem will not go away.

<u>Action possibilities</u>   Formulate new strategies
to influence senior managers.
Reconstrue and adapt - leave time (at home?)
to do the work.
Examine overall time-management.
Enlist support of colleagues to pressure for
more resources.

I thought Eleanor looked relaxed and well when I
met her for the feedback meeting.  I commented on
this and she smiled, saying that she would 'tell me
about that soon'.  She received my feedback, giving
many positive non-verbal responses.  She listened
without interrupting, and then talked expansively.
Between our meetings, she said, she had decided that
her reactions to her clerical problems were vastly
exaggerated in her mind, and that she could easily
manage to work at home to cover the difficulties.
Moreover, she now found that other problems she had
thought about - particularly some difficult working
relationships - had suddenly fallen into perspective.  She regarded herself as quite able to improve
matters - <u>she</u> bore some of the responsibility for
the difficulties.

The immediate beneficial effects of the counselling were plain to see, and intrigued Eleanor:

'I'm fascinated that by sharing that issue
with you - which has been going on a long
time - a hell of a lot suddenly came together.  Says a lot about the need to talk to
people who are quite outside the organisation.'

I shared in Eleanor's emotional 'high', but I was
concerned that her self-discoveries should be placed
upon a more permanent footing to enable her to
tackle any new stresses (which indeed were to arise
in our four further meetings).  Eleanor was an
introspective person and was anxious to discover
some of the roots of her difficulties.  Appropriate
help appeared to be in providing her with an opportunity to clarify the dimensions of her problems so
that she could work with them in her own way.  She
regarded experimenting with her life style as an

important challenge, and if I could stimulate that challenge she would seriously act in a way she felt appropriate to the management of stress.

Thus, the feedback session moved away from Eleanor's cathartic reactions to a close examination of her reasons for perceiving certain problems as threatening. I focussed her attention on the personality and self themes that had emerged from the stress analysis, and our discussion intensified around her desire to influence and control events - which she recognised could become self-defeating as she rarely achieved the control she desired. Were her control expectations unrealisable?

'My problem of control is a life problem. It's fundamental. My illnesses are a loss of control. I'm trying to get myself together in a number of ways - like taking holidays without feeling delinquent and acting in advance of anticipated problems, rather than my characteristic crisis response. This is a considerable breakthrough for me, and I'll try to keep it up!'

In sum, my work with Eleanor had more immediate impact, and was ultimately more influential in self-development, than with John or Diana. Her emphasis had shifted from concern about a tangible work problem (which was not to re-emerge), to why such a problem should feel threatening. The intrapsychic issues were the ones that were most important to her, and I could help point them out. Her intended action was to use her own analytic skills, and the emotional support of others (especially her religious community), to re-direct her attitudes and beliefs more 'healthily', less stressfully.

ONGOING STRESS ANALYSES

Many of the stress analyses were introduced less formally than the ones mentioned so far, during a plateau in Phase II exploration. This was obviously necessary when a second meeting appeared unlikely; but, also, it could fit the direction of the moment - when a problem area was well explored and the next logical, and psychological, step was to focus on action plans.

My feedback and action-structuring occurred in various ways according to the issues presented, and how 'ready' the individual seemed. The following extracts give some indication of what I did:

Home Help Organiser: 'I was overwhelmed with work when the crisis blew up in my face. They gave lipservice to the load problem here, but no more. There's always "financial difficulties". I don't think anyone realises the amount of work that has to be done. No one's ever sitting with you. I'm so very worried about such a crisis happening again.'

Me: 'How can you reduce the risk of it happening, and protect yourself a bit more?'

Home Help Organiser: 'I am my worst enemy, but I can't help the type of person I am. I don't know how to protect myself. Possibly by involving my supervisor more. Demanding. I'm not demanding.'

Me: 'This may be the key. I get the feeling you are protecting your supervisor because you see him so stressed - but you are the one who loses out in the end by not using him.'

Home Help Organiser: 'I could certainly push for the supervision I need. I do so need someone else to help get rid of my problems and tensions. This is what my supervisor should be doing for me.'

Me: 'You could make a firm promise to yourself to get him, or someone else, to take on some of the problems. Can you reasonably expect yourself to hold on to them all?'

Home Help Organiser: 'I can see this. Also, another route is through regular meetings or "surgeries" with my home helps, say once a month, to clear the air. I've let them drop away, which has left me with more pressure: they are constantly wanting my individual attention.'

Me: 'How could you set this up?'

----------

Social Worker: 'It's the plans for the new organisation. Sets up vague fears for me. There's no mention of intake in the new plans, which <u>really</u> threatens me. I'm always worried I'm going to end up doing something else. I like the adolescent kids on intake. I like the variety, plus the opportunity to focus on cases.'

Me: 'A number of times you have given me the strong impression of how powerless you are in these sorts of situations. Maybe you are. On the other hand, could it be that you've convinced yourself that you can't do anything, when you actually do have some power and influence?'

Social Worker: 'Well ... I sit in meetings and feel my blood pressure rising. My team leader doesn't really <u>listen</u> to what people are saying. I also get <u>this</u> feeling when I feel pushed by a medical man into signing a compulsory order for a client's hospital treatment <u>against</u> my better judgement. I've never really analysed why this gets to me. Maybe I'm too much of a coward and I don't stand up for what I really want.'

Me: 'I get the sense of a deep anger because you have failed your self in some way; for not doing what you <u>feel</u> is right.'

Social Worker: 'Yes. And ironically I know I <u>can</u> support my position because there is, deep down, a campaigning bit of me that I need to use.'

Me: 'Maybe that campaigning bit can re-emerge to help you in these situations? What does it look like?'

----------

In each of these cases I was moving the individual towards acknowledging certain sources of threat while encouraging and reinforcing particular action possibilities. All this happened 'in flow', using what I saw to be important stress data that had been presented to me. In such improvised analyses I would make connections across the full discussion up to that point if it helped to illuminate a situation. Consequently the recurrent 'powerless' theme in the second case was one that I felt to be important, stress-relevant.

Some social workers had reached their own fairly clear views about the causes and possible solutions to their personal stress problems, and wanted to talk about them. I would assist them in re-examining their analyses, if necessary encouraging them to look at their difficulties from other perspectives, and then helping them to specify action plans. One example of this type was a social worker who had decided to seek alternative supervision. The relationship with his existing supervisor was an unhappy one. As the supervisor was a team leader, the social worker wondered whether he was more interested in appeasing senior managers than representing his staff. Over the years the social worker's mistrust had grown, and he cited a number of instances which supported his feelings. He had now started discussions with his colleagues for peer supervision.

I discovered that he had so far failed to address the political ramifications of this move. What would be his team leader's position? Would the Area Director be involved? Would he create longer-term difficulties for himself? We talked over these questions at length and reviewed strategies for making the move he desired as smooth and painless as possible.

Ongoing stress analyses were sometimes appropriate for individuals who had experienced a recent crisis. For example, two participants were depressed and anxious about their 'failures' in recent promotion interviews. To some extent both were in a state of shock and disorientation. They talked of their inadequacy, resentment, lost pride, and purposelessness. To help them release some of their anger and tension I encouraged as much open conversation (Phase II) as possible, before considering more focussed action. I asked them about their feelings before, during and after the promotion interview, their previous career plans, and the effect of the situation on their life in general. In both cases I was able to gradually turn their own reflections and

reactions back on themselves to help them see more
clearly why they were feeling as they did, and where
they could move next. Initially, the best data I
had for such purposes were their own responses to
their disappointment - which were diametrically
opposite in form. One cast all the blame for the
outcome on himself. Somehow, he felt, he should
have managed the situation better - more accurately
anticipated the content of the promotion interview.
The other saw 'the villains' as the senior management team who, in his opinion, had quite misjudged
him - they had been 'manifestly unfair'.

I observed (openly) that their reactions were
probably ways of coping with their sense of injury,
a form of self protection. But these activities
were not working too well - the threat to their
pride and competence was still lingering on in an
apparently unresolvable fashion. It was unlikely
that there was a single source of blame for their
difficulties.

In their own ways they gradually began to step out
of their remorse. Our discussions turned towards
the vagaries and politics of promotion, and the way
that our expectations can become unrealistically
shaped when something is very important to us. I
encouraged them to take stock of their current position and fortunes, and look for ways of developing
their present jobs (rather than dwell upon the possible benefits of a job they had not obtained).

There were a few participants who, unlike those
mentioned so far, resisted any moves towards action
planning. This could occur when the stress 'problem' was firmly embedded in a much broader life-
stress syndrome reflecting ingrained fears, inadequacies or anxieties. My 'ping pong' conversation
with one social worker nicely illustrates this
situation:

Me: 'Do you take initiatives before you get so
    terribly overloaded. Specify to your super-
    visor just what you can and cannot take on?'

Social Worker: 'No. I can't do it. I've really
    tried to say "no" in the last fortnight, but
    he won't take it from me. I can't even say
    "no" to my husband!'

Me: 'Maybe we could work out a new way of approaching your supervisor.'

Social Worker: 'There's no point. I've tried lots of things and it only causes rancour.'

Me: 'I get the feeling that the major growth for you would be to move to a position where you feel you are doing your job well and moving on to carve out your own work patterns. Your good work gets all mixed up with the authority issues.'

Social Worker: 'Yes, but I just get reprimanded for doing anything like this.'

Me: 'Perhaps we could begin to think why you always feel this way. What's behind it.'

Social Worker: 'Oh - I'll never lose this thing I have about those in authority.'

Interactions of this sort happened with four people. They did want to talk about their 'impossible' situation, a process which they described as helpful. However they were reluctant to disturb the 'roots' of their difficulties - and it is perhaps questionable how much one should (or counselling can) disturb them. Most of them were far more comfortable and responsive in talking about ways of managing their anxieties - breaks from work, exercise routines and forms of relaxation.

# 11  Action and support

Half of the group moved on to the final counselling phase - turning action plans into specific changes of behaviour or belief. I worked in two ways. The first (and least frequent) method was through my direct, physical involvement in the social worker's problem solving: I would play a personal part in the process. The second was more distant, less engaged. The full responsibility for taking action was the social worker's, but I would help to review his or her progress and, if necessary, re-set action plans. Some illustrations of these approaches will provide a clearer picture of what I did.

DIRECT INTERVENTION

The following two interventions indicate some of the variations in my role for rather different problem situations.

David

David, a senior social worker, was very concerned about what he viewed as his poor ability at managing personal confrontations - direct negotiations with senior members of his own organisation and officers in other agencies: 'When I'm caught unprepared I feel under attack. It's my most anxious period. Can I handle myself better - more skilfully?' I agreed to help him. First of all he would ask his team leader to observe his confrontational behaviour in actual work meetings for a period of two weeks. Then I would help them discuss the implications of the observations, and also look at how any discoveries we made could be used for developing new behaviours or skills.

The observations revealed David's almost overzealous need to 'win' in his interactions, which made him aggressive and defensive, and in practice reduced his power to influence others, or successfully negotiate. Could he 'lose' sometimes, and save face? What if he tried a less forthright approach? David was keen to experiment with different styles, but in a safe setting. So I suggested a second activity - a simulated case study where I would act as his foil. His team leader scripted the roles, which were primed for confrontation. I was David's 'boss' who had suspended one of his favoured colleagues for 'irregular' behaviour with a client, behaviour that I alone knew about. David was to act as an aggrieved friend determined to get me to reverse my 'unfair' decision. (We were unaware of each other's roles before the simulation.) In the role-play David struggled to move beyond his rather taut, aggressive style. When he was able to, I could find space to listen to his arguments and explore his position with him. I also felt more able to reveal my 'secret' information. We shared our impressions, and David claimed to find change difficult, but possible. Some weeks later his team leader commented that he was continuing to 'improve', and working hard to do so.

This intervention was aimed at influencing interpersonal skills within a role, and was less involved with the psychodynamic reasons for David's 'need to win'. It was evident to me, and to David, that there was scope for possible change at the former level, but not the latter.

Directing attention to role behaviour was also the rationale behind my work with Diana and Alan - the second example of my direct intervention.

## Diana and Alan

Diana's problems working with Alan have been described in Chapter 10. I considered it important to structure a way of helping them to discover, and review, their perceptions of each other's role behaviours. I did this by a form of 'role negotiation' (Harrison, 1972). In our first joint meeting I asked them to list features of the other person's role behaviour that helped them in their own effectiveness, and then list those aspects that hindered their effectiveness. We then identified 'negotiable' items - areas that each of them felt they would like to talk about and maybe change. Diana's attempts to review and reformulate their styles of working were at first accepted by Alan; but after a while, as the full extent of her anxieties became clear, Alan reacted in surprise and shock. He was unprepared for the depth of her concerns, and the apparent gulf between them. He became defensive - the scene was just too much for him to comprehend so suddenly.

I eased the meeting to a close to allow some settling period for Alan. Meanwhile I met him separately to discuss his new anxieties and help him through what was clearly a painful realisation that there was much turbulence around him of which he had been unaware.

Our second joint meeting began in a reasonably relaxed fashion. I talked a little about Alan's reactions to the process, and he claimed to feel easier having spoken to me and also having talked with Diana before the meeting. The divergence in their styles of working was recreated in detail in this meeting, encouraged by myself. Indeed Alan declared that he now saw a dramatic philsophical difference between them - which was 'important' for him to know. At this fundamental level they could find no meeting point - 'but maybe we could find different ways of working when I've thought about it more' said Alan. Where they could, and did, make some progress was in agreeing some new administrative arrangements in the work, which would benefit them both. They discussed details and target dates for change. Diana declared that she was pleased and relieved to have gone through the whole process as it had opened dialogue between them - although some

of the fundamental issues between them remained
unresolved.


INDIRECT INTERVENTION

Most of the social workers I met in the final phase
of counselling had left our previous meeting with
the intention to act for themselves in some agreed
way. I was now seeing them again to review their
progress. My work with three people - Ann, Jim and
Martin - provides a flavour of the types of directions that they, and I, took.

Ann

Between meetings Ann looked into her client files to
try to identify some of the characteristics of those
clients she found to be 'emotionally taxing', and
those who did not have that effect on her. This
arose from our earlier work where she talked of the
emotional costs of her child-care activities. There
was the 'enormous responsibility' of taking a child
into care, or sending it back to foster parents.
'How can I be sure I'm right?' Added to this were
clear attachments to certain children - an emotional
involvement that she felt 'had to happen', but left
her confused in her decision making. 'I miss out
the logical bits - get emotional and angry with
myself.' Yet, what puzzled her was why she felt
some clients were so stressful, and others were not.
If she could understand this better, maybe, she
thought, she could cope better.

   Despite complaints of 'an enormous load', Ann
found time to sort through her files and bring some
with her to our action follow-up meeting. I encouraged her to look at four in detail - two which
had stressed her, and two which had not, and to
describe to me some of the differences. From this
process we identified a number of characteristics
which, perhaps not surprisingly, reflected on herself as much as her clients. For example, she
identified closely with children whom she liked -
what happened to them was felt almost as an exten-
sion of herself. Her loss of control of children to
an institution or another party was fraught with
mutual separation anxiety, especially if she did not
like what was happening to them.

There were frequent manifestations of the insecurity and lack of confidence of someone new to social work, learning their way; and a certain desperation to care and protect vulnerable, and attractive, youngsters. On hearing this from me, she commented:

'Yes, and I'm super conscious about my age with older children. I'm not old enough to be a mother figure or young enough to be an elder sister, so I don't know what role I'm supposed to be playing with older kids. The younger kid is a more natural relationship. It's a bit frightening. Am I doing them as much good as I think?'

Yet her general unease melted away when I asked her to tell me how she coped with 'low stress' cases. It was as if another 'Ann' emerged who could coolly distance, or cut off, clients - particularly adult ones - who 'depressed her too much' or were overdependent on her.

Ann's actions, and my review with her, gave her insights into her stresses, and identified influences which up until then appeared uncontrollable. She remarked that now she would be able to articulate the reasons for her feelings more clearly to supportive colleagues, and also be more self-conscious about identifying and managing potential high stress, 'involving' clients.

Jim

Jim was the only social worker I talked to who declared acute financial difficulties, a problem he found to be affecting almost every sphere of his life. He had recently completed training with, he claimed, very little assistance from his employers. He had had to use all of his limited savings to help meet his training costs and removal expenses:

'I do feel the Authority have given me a rough deal, especially the Personnel Department. I'm married, with a family, and on a rock bottom salary. I'm not that interested in money! I devote much of my time to my work, but I don't want to worry about money. I'm now feeling apathetic and lethargic - no energy.'

After much discussion we had decided that it was worth him entering his 'lion's den' - the Personnel Department - to plead his special case:

'I haven't done this. Most people get a rough ride from them. But it does make a lot of sense! It's worth a try. It's direct, and an opportunity for picking up a more varied view of the situation - rather than getting things distorted through lots of different people. I'll do it.'

He did not do it. He explained to me, in the follow-up meeting, that our action-focussing had sparked off a totally new approach to his problem. It occurred to him that his wife, also a social worker in the organisation, probably had more chance of improving her salary prospects than he had. He knew of posts available that could give her a higher salary. Together they approached the appropriate Assistant Director with their views. To their delight, he responded sympathetically and 'found a way of re-grading her'.

My help for Jim was patently oblique. The content of our agreed action was less significant than the motivating influence of going through that process. This had stimulated Jim to create a new direction for himself while setting aside his remorse and scapegoating of 'the system'. He had managed to re-engage a proactive style of problem solving - which was far more typical of his usual work behaviour.

Martin

Martin, my last example, also failed to carry out his intended action plan. But this time the reason was because it turned out to be an inappropriate plan, and my challenge was to help him find a better one.

In Phase III Martin revealed a deep frustration, anger and impatience with the growing piles of paperwork on his desk. Not only did he feel impotent to tackle and organise such work (a feeling that he had had for many months), he now found that it threatened his self-esteem in a number of ways. He felt vulnerable about being discovered as 'inefficient' and 'incompetent' by colleagues and supervisors. More and more he was making excuses for work not done, constantly retrieving situations because of his own lack of action. He was putting in longer and longer hours, and much evening work, but now late work was becoming less possible because of the demands of a young family at home.

There was a growing feeling of impending crisis, coupled with a certain desperation of not knowing what to do, but recognising that something had to be done. 'It is too easy to say "that is the person I am" ' he claimed, 'it is a cop out. People can ask, with every justification - does the fact that you have not written anything mean that you have not done anything? There has to be <u>some</u> improvement.

We talked at length about his fears of reprobation and censure from his supervisor should he declare the problem to him. He offered little to substantiate his worries and admitted that 'maybe things have got way out of perspective. I really have to talk to him and get his help and support - and I will!' We agreed that I would review his progress with this at our next meeting. That meeting began with a confession:

> 'Well, nothing really has happened since we last met. We talked of sharing it with my supervisor, but I haven't done it. My fault, I suppose. So the problem is still there. But I haven't deliberately not seen him.'

I considered it most important to try and discover what had prevented him carrying out his intentions, especially if some plausible alternative action was to be found. In doing this he revealed a new dimension in his relationship with his supervisor. Martin had recently failed in an application for promotion and he felt his supervisor had contributed to this. Therefore he was very wary about confiding in his supervisor in case his trust would be betrayed at a later date, and used against him. This information cast a different complexion on feasible action.

I suggested that maybe we could find a way of starting on his paperwork without seeking help elsewhere. He balked at this. There were 'obstacles' like lack of privacy in his room, little time, his poor writing ability. I chose to challenge these rather than collude with them, offering possibilities to meet each apparent difficulty. He gradually conceded that he was maybe looking for excuses because of the overwhelming size of the task. I responded:

'Look - why don't you diary right now a half-day a week for nothing but report writing. Shut yourself away outside of your office - in this room, in a library, at home, anywhere. But don't let anything else cut into that time. I'll see you in two weeks time to see how you've done.'

He looked surprised, and a little meek, at my direct approach. He said that he probably could do that if he tried. He would try. In our next meeting he looked elated. He had had a whole day at his paperwork and it was now under control. He said he now felt every reason to continue that routine - a point which I reinforced, thoroughly.

# Concluding points

The social workers' views about the counselling - expressed during the process and in their written comments eight weeks later, varied.  Many referred to the welcome attention from 'an interested outsider', although the main impact of the event was judged more in terms of the severity of their pre-senting stress problems.  So some claimed little change because 'my problems were not great', or 'I really wanted to give you my general impressions of stress here'.  Others, though (some 60 per cent), described quite profound personal changes.

   The case accounts and extracts in Chapters 10 and 11 reveal some of the counselling outcomes.  An overall picture indicates the following effects:

- Reconstruing perceived problems; a redefini-tion of urgency and threat.
- Increased self awareness
- A reformulation of work methods and roles.
- New, or renewed, dialogue with key colleagues or other staff.
- Re-assigning responsibility and re-asserting authority.
- Developing support networks within and beyond the workplace.
- Shifting from defensive to proactive coping.

- Feelings of ease, lightness, and catharsis.
- Developing new interactional skills.
- Renewed confidence to confront old problems.
- Extending protective defences.
- Assessing the role of past stress for present coping.
- New forms of time management.
- Planned recreation and relaxation.

Some of these were described as an immediate consequence of the counselling - such as cathartic feelings, self awareness, new confidence, and re-defining problems. Most of the others happened within the eight-week period following specific action to alter a task, procedure or relationship.

The 'permanence' of the counselling effects is hard to judge. Some stress problems were self-contained and specific to a particular situation - their solution was viewed as an end in itself. But there were social workers who described changes in their attitudes and styles of coping which trans-cended their difficulties at the time of the counselling. Beyond this, the beneficial effects are likely to vary according to how much reinforcing support a social worker wants and gets. The organi-sation offered no continuing resources akin to my own role.

It was remarkable, observed some social workers, that anything at all had happened through our work together, especially when their problems had 'festered so long', and I had no formal organisa-tional authority to influence them. I think a number of features coalesced in this respect. Firstly, the social workers' curiosity or need was a major ingredient in our meeting - a reasonable basis for their further commitment and one which provided me with a good start if I was going to influence them. Secondly, my informal position in the organi-sation, beholden to no other person, freed them and myself from 'accountability' posturing and defences. We were not glancing anxiously over our shoulders, worried about how our activities might be seen by others in the organisation. Thirdly, there was a seductiveness in the role I was playing. I could not be accused of 'social working' them because I was neither a social worker nor their colleague. However, my activities were not unlike some of theirs, and for them to receive attention in this way was a novel, if not startling experience. As Smith (1978) cogently notes, a personal counselling service remains a dream for most social workers.

Finally, there is the power and impact of 'stopping the music'. This is, to some extent, a characteristic of most social research, but in this study it was particularly accentuated. When a social worker was with me he or she could not do any work, could not be interrupted, and could not rely on accustomed ways of interaction. The props and distractions of normal work routines were temporarily suspended, an ambiguous situation where self becomes more naked and unprotected. In these circumstances it is hard not to confront oneself to some extent; taken-for-granted assumptions are implicitly and explicitly challenged.

The confidential, capsule-like, atmosphere of the counselling also needs to be viewed against the network of interrelationships that may form part of an individual's stress problems. To act for one person can expose an 'innocent' other. One case in this study, the partnership of Diana and Alan, nicely illustrates how an intervention at Diana's instigation raised issues for Alan which were far from benign, confronting him with difficulties he never knew existed. The run-on effects from one person's change to another may be difficult or impossible to judge, but they become hard (and in my view unethical) to ignore when a specific relationship forms part of one person's stress problem. It is an odd position, to say the least, for the improvement in one person's stress to be matched by a steep increase in another's, without some attempt to handle the 'whole' situation (Warwick, 1981; Fineman and Mclean, 1984).

# Part IV
# The wider scene and
# implications

# 12 A wider look

The picture which has emerged from this study is necessarily a part portrayal of the stress experiences of social workers, restricted to snapshots of a particular group within a short-to-moderate time frame. Nevertheless, there is strong reason to believe that what was declared was central to the workers' well-being and often at the heart of their very survival in the organisation. The research contract and relationship released many candid perceptions, including admissions of vulnerability and inadequacy which, as far as I can judge, were not spoken elsewhere, or if they were, were re-packaged to appear less personal, more socially desirable.

How typical are such stress experiences? What additional insights are available from studies of field-workers in other British local authority settings? These questions can normally be addressed from published research - but unfortunately there is not a great deal to work from in the present case. A search of the social science literature reveals few directly comparable studies, and none that use an intervention approach. Nevertheless, three works, each quite detailed in scope, are important yardsticks for us to consider.

A major qualitative, interview study on the nature of social work practice in local authority social services teams was conducted by Stevenson and Parsloe (1978). Their researchers contacted 360 social work staff across the United Kingdom, including a number from psychiatric and general hospitals. They explored ten broad areas identified by pilot work as 'crucial' to social work activity. These included features of work content, supervision, specialisation and, especially pertinent to our purpose, 'pressures on social workers'. Their study does not claim to move deeply into the dynamics of stress and coping, and the concept of pressure is employed in a fairly gross form. Furthermore, by incorporating the social worker's own 'corrections' to the data, undertaken in the knowledge that the research report would be seen by their director, a certain blunting and censorship of the more personal, sensitive information might be expected. Nevertheless, aspects of their findings show a considerable concordance with the essence, if not the detail, of some of those in the present study - in particular, the anxieties associated with the following:

- The unpredictability and fluctuations of work and the urgent demands which constantly interrupt the organisation of work. The sheer overall volume was less of an issue than its unpredictability.

- The constant dilemma as to where to put one's energies. Children at risk? Visiting established clients? Crisis visits?

- Fears over responsibility for people in trouble, especially children. Dealing with people's lives, not objects or things. Doubts over whether a decision on a child or old person is the right one. The fear of public exposure in a crisis.

- Attachments to certain clients, and the difficulties in handling clients' overbearing expectations of social work. Being torn by conflicting demands from different members of a client family: helping one person can harm another.

- The tension between being a generic or specialist social worker, and the helplessness in the face of unfamiliar types of client.

148

- Social work assistants' ambiguity of role and responsibility, and their uncertain status.

- The social worker's sharp alienation from head-quarters and senior management - they were there to be confronted for resources.

- The price of lonely responsibility paid by those who worked independently of formal super-vision. Informal peer support was important to some, but avoided by others.

- Feeling the repository for so many of society's problems.

The researchers also observed an apparent apoliti-cality of team members, with little coherent purpose to influence higher management policy. The 'radical' social worker was a rare animal. Little inter-team communication was recorded, a likely reflection of the privatisation of work. Indeed, the prevalence of privatisation lent a certain fiction to the notion of 'team' work, the actual work emanating from an individual case-worker repor-ting, to a lesser or greater extent, to a senior. Privatisation was also viewed as a self-protective, defensive device, insulating the worker from team tension. But this tension, and the whole team climate, was markedly influenced by the personal style and charisma of the team leader. These quali-ties were considerably more important than the leader's formal authority, and there was evidence of collusion amongst workers to deny such authority.

Satyamurti 's (1981) participant observation study of two local authority teams is more intensely focussed on how individuals cope with the pressures of their job. It is a sociologically inspired inves-tigation of 40 social workers, and includes perspec-tives from some clients and observers outside of social work. Like Stevenson and Parsloe's use of pressure, Satyamurti employs stress more as a broad-ly descriptive, rather than analytic, category. This makes it difficult at times to disentangle the nature of differences in response in her generalist reporting. Her conclusion that stress is an inevi-table consequence of the current structural features of social work, independent of the personalities of team members, is more radical than, but not unlike, Stevenson and Parsloe's contention that stress is

inherent in the social worker role. These are deba-
table views, to which I will return in the next
chapter.

Satyamurti's account of her findings certainly
provides illuminating points of intersection with
both the present study and Stevenson and Parsloe's.
The possessiveness and privatisation of work emerges
once again, which Satyamurti regards as a necessary
consequence of the statutory responsibility which
attends interaction with a client. Such a relationship confuses the care and control functions of the
work, she argues, imposing an emotional burden on
the social worker which can be partly relieved
through peer contact. Peer support provides recip-
rocated attention to anxieties and frustrations and
creates a safe region of contact, delineating boundaries and identifying 'enemies' - especially headquarters. The rules of such support proscribe the
'case working' of a colleague and consider those who
contract out as marginal team members. Peer interaction of this sort was markedly more effective than
the support of seniors, who rarely met the social
workers' expectations. Nevertheless, 'overuse' of a
senior could trigger peer sanctions - the offending
social worker acquiring a reputation for helplessness and dependence.

Satyamurti's social workers, like those in the
other groups, were struggling with the oppression of
a relentless and fragmented workload. There was the
heavy weight of responsibility accentuated by 'life-
or-death' decisions. She proposes that the emotional quality of relationships compensated to some
extent for the indeterminate nature of success with
clients: creating a pleasant atmosphere with
clients, and investing in peer relationships, provided some sense of meaning and achievement in the
work, no matter how peripheral. Other ways of
coping with anxiety ranged from the protective
institutional response 'it could happen to anyone'
when crisis or disaster hit a particular worker, to
specific avoidance behaviours - such as busily
occupying oneself with office work rather than visiting a client, taking unofficial time off, going
sick, seeking promotion away from client contact, or
resigning.

The evenly balanced relationship with a client was
far less evident than the lopsided one of 'parent-

child', an inequality maintained by a social work vocabulary which readily categorised the client as helpless, immature or recalcitrant. Yet such defensive distancing on the part of the social worker contained the irony that client-disapproved behaviour paralleled much of the worker's own behaviour in the oganisation. Each appeared helpless in their own right. Satyamurti observed a '... gross and pervasive insensitivity to the feelings of clients children were received into care. Yet, more generally, work with children, and with families, was seen to be more rewarding than geriatric care, where client independence was a depressingly rare outcome.

A final point concerns the allocation of work. This was based less on a worker's status or specific skill than on how that person's anxiety-tolerance was perceived. A senior would allocate work to whoever seemed able to cope with further load, an expedience which left many inexperienced social workers and social work assistants with a more demanding caseload than their more experienced counterparts.

Social worker survival and anxiety was one aspect of Mattinson and Sinclair's (1979) broader analysis of marital case work in a local authority. They gathered data on 68 clients - married couples - some from their own activity with them and some from that of other workers. There are some now familiar themes in their findings: the pressures from the excessive quantity and variety of work; the bureaucratic constraints of their department; the heightened seriousness of events surrounding clients; feeling helpless in the face of seemingly impossible client demands; conflicts with, and condescension from, other professionals; and a generally hostile social environment which placed high and idealised expectations upon them. The authors observed three forms of coping, or techniques of survival. The first was to restrict the load at intake stage by avoiding all requests other than those with clear statutory implications, or those where urgent help was viewed as absolutely critical for the client. This, though, had the net effect of increasing the onerousness of the load. Secondly, social workers would attempt to smother their anxieties about work purpose and client relationships by behaving in a hectic, crisis-driven manner - to 'get the job done'. This pattern, the authors note, mirrored their clients' behaviour in many ways, and was often just as ineffective at anxiety protection: the social workers sensed an omnipresent vulnerability and fear of catastrophe, and became considerably depressed with their lack of progress with certain clients. They could escape their impotence by a third form of coping - avoiding client contact. Given the lack of clear pointers as to how best to work with emotional problems, social workers fumbled, '... to dabble with them in uncertain, undefined, and unreliable ways' (p. 295). This proved very hard to live with, so sometimes it felt better to not try at all.

The above studies, although of different emphasis to the present one, suggest that the range of stress sources and experiences in this study are not untypical of the experiences of local authority fieldworkers. It is a picture which is reinforced also by other studies of local authority social work - such as in residential settings, intake activity, and general surveys of the work (Dunham, 1980, 1981; Mawby, 1979; Prodgers, 1979). But let us broaden the comparative context a little further by looking briefly at the social worker stress literature outside of local authority organisations, to include non-British research.

THE BROADER LITERATURE

The general literature on social worker stress is dominated by American research, particularly on burnout. The studies range from the speculative to the specific and hypothesis-based. Psychometric and survey methodology is far more common than systematic qualitative analysis. I do not intend a comprehensive, detailed review of this work, but propose to highlight those themes which qualify or elaborate the findings so far.

In the present study, burnout is regarded as an end-piece to the stress process, a view supported by a number of writers in the field (e.g. Paine, 1982; Sweeney, 1981). Yet these same writers also note that burnout has tended not to be integrated into the stress literature, a position further complicated by the association of burnout with different psychological processes - such as job dissatisfaction, disillusionment or alienation (Cherniss, 1980;

Maslach, 1982). Whatever psychological phenomenon best characterises burnout will no doubt continue to be debated, although its adaptive/defensive quality makes it a very strong contender for stress. But the argument over the proper place for burnout is perhaps overshadowed by the toing and froing of views on the causes of burnout - intrapersonal, interpersonal, organisational, societal, or some mix of these. One's position in this argument is more than academic when ameliorative action or change is proposed - a point to which I return in the final chapter.

The pervasiveness of burnout is unclear. The reader of the mainstream literature could be forgiven for assuming, from its tone, that all social workers and the like are on the path to chronic stress and inevitable burnout on joining the profession. Certainly, some of the social workers' own norms of practice seemed to edge them in this direction - such as the oft early-communicated expectation that social workers will burnout in the first year, and 'support' groups which reinforce such feelings through carping, sarcasm and hostility (Shannon and Saleebey, 1980). But few studies provide a sense of perspective on the incidence of burnout, and those that do show that it is confined to a modest proportion, 11 per cent or less (Pines and Kafry, 1978; Streepy, 1981). There is a hint that the ten per cent located in this sample may not unduly misrepresent the actual proportion within the group. Where burnout/chronic stress is likely to occur the most susceptible have been described as: the younger, inexperienced, poorly supported workers; in inappropriate specialisms; in over centralised bureaucracies, with large case loads; low in autonomy; in ambiguous roles; led by insufficiently structuring leaders; and caught in economic constraints (Armstrong, 1979; Eldridge et al, 1983; Lewis, 1980; McNeely, 1983; Pines and Kafry, 1978; Streepy, 1981). These 'risk factors', many of which were identified in one form or another in the present study, can presumably combine in many different ways, and all be present for some less fortunate souls. One clustering was clear in this study - the inadequately supported newly qualified worker, struggling with a load ill matched in quantity and quality to his or her experience or capacity.

The client role in stress and burnout receives considerable attention in the literature. There are many corroborative findings: anxiety over babies and children; client dependency and over-identification with the client; the overwhelming depths of the client's needs; intractability of some client problems; liked and disliked clients; violent clients; the client's power to hurt the social worker; the client's enormous expectations of the social worker; and the intense avalanche of feeling confronting the social worker (Addison, 1980; Barrett and McKelvey, 1980; Carpenter, 1977; Dunham, 1981; Maslach, 1978; Mayer and Rosenblatt, 1975; Niehouse, 1983; Pines and Maslach, 1978). Less familiar, in terminology at least, is the client's love or hate for the social worker, emphasised by Tonnesman (1979). In the present study, there were clear allusions to certain clients who found the social worker's presence unacceptable, or resented their intervention - such as in the enforcement of a child care order. Open, or thinly disguised, hate may have been not far away in these circumstances. But no social worker confessed to the 'nuisance of a passionately loving client' (Tonnesman, 1979, p.36). Perhaps experiences of this sort were just too sensitive to reveal - although the affections and emotional attachments of children were freely expressed.

The social worker's ambivalence, and discomfort, towards power in relationship to the client, touched on in my own and Satayamurti's work, is given an interesting perspective by Carpenter (1977). She argues that part of the social worker's power derives from the more general phenomenon of the high credibility of a passing stranger to the person who is lost; a relatively calm individual in a messy situation. Yet the social worker is loath to admit owning or using such power, fearful of the manipulative, negative implications it might suggest, in particular 'power' to hurt pople. It is safer to believe that the relationship is rationally and openly balanced, right from the start.

Research on the perceived local and broader organisational sources of stress is rather less than that on client issues; yet, once again, the principal findings overlap considerably with those of this study. They include: the intrusion of paperwork and administration; office politics which slow down or block responses to clients; tension between colleagues; the lack of tangible indices of success; little positive feedback or encouragement from the organisation; vulnerability to public criticism; difficulties in courts of law; and the broader social and political pressure on social workers to achieve results which seem impossible in relation to their modest resources (Daley, 1979; Edelwich and Brodsky, 1980; Niehouse, 1983; Pines and Kafry, 1978; Tonnesman, 1979).

The invidious position of the social worker, set squarely at the impact point between social structures and the citizen in distress, is debated vigorously in the literature (see Brewer and Lait, 1980; Pearson, 1975; Watson, 1979). Should the social worker act to change 'the system' or help its victims? In its polarised form, this dilemma appears to exercise commentators on social work more than the majority of workers themselves: the business of surviving with clients, and the daily melee of the office, consumes most of their available energy. Coping with statutory and bureaucratic demands, though, is viewed as a critical ingredient in survival, to the extent that humanitarian concerns are edged aside, or eroded. The social worker is pushed to classify and proceduralise in order to protect self and system, often at the cost of reduced client contact and concern. The extent of humanistic, caring drive in social workers, or 'dedicatory ethic' (Kadushin, 1974) is, as already argued, a moot point. Whatever does exist, however, is certainly straitjacketed by such organisational logic, and is further challenged by what Watson (1979) observes as the scientific/objective vocabulary of contemporary social work - a language which insulates the worker from a close (and potentially stressful) human encounter, obviating the need for a high degree of empathic involvement. The defensive coping, so prominent in the present study, is highlighted in the general literature where a range of diversionary/distancing defences are described, such as: stereotyping clients; avoiding visiting new clients; 'wasting' time between client visits; following the letter of decision rules; blaming clients for their condition; depersonalising/dehumanising clients; relying heavily upon others; and mechanising conversations with clients (Armstrong, 1979; Pines and Kafry, 1978; Pines and Maslach, 1978; Tonnesman, 1979; Watson, 1979).

Concerning non-work sources of social worker stress, there is a conspicuous absence of conceptualisation and research of this type - a somewhat ironical position for those who look to the wider structures and systems to account for stress and survival. There is only one study I can trace, by Barrett and McKelvey (1980), which makes some acknowledgement of this issue. They adapt Adams' (1978) stress framework to provide a stress 'checklist' for social workers. On this they include a few 'life change' items, but ones not grounded in social workers' experiences. Taylor-Brown et al (1981) undertake a similar Adams-inspired listing, but puzzlingly omit non-work sources.

# 13 Stress and intervention: some reflections

In this final chapter I wish to highlight some implications of the main findings, and their broader context. I am selecting a few areas which have particular significance for me in what they suggest about understanding and acting upon social worker stress.

## MEANING AND PURPOSE

In a work world of often ambiguous purpose and hazy success, social workers cling to whatever they can create as meaningful or purposeful: the short term gains of intake work, the gratitude of the elderly, the growing independence of child clients, the warmth of client and colleague relationships, the power over clients, the cat and mouse tussles with other agencies or management staff, .... and so on. Yet these psychic anchors can be unreliable, sometimes ephemeral: there is the omnipresent threat that work and effort will turn out to be futile, purposeless. Any statement of 'primary task' in social work should be considered against these experienced realities. Such a statement, say through executive or managerial dictum, may be a convenient and important fiction - it creates a semblance of rational purpose to management, to social workers, and perhaps to clients. But actual social worker behaviour will be pushed and pulled in many directions, often quite unrelated to the 'ideal purpose'. And herein lie the seeds of stress.

Creating purpose in social work cannot be fully appreciated without some notion as to what social workers may be groping towards. Meanings will be generated in reactions to circumstances, but this process is directed in part by features of personality and biography. The pervasive 'caring, helping others' tag enshrined in handbooks of social work seems a half truth - as much an oversimplification or camouflage of what a social worker wants to do or be as an accurate reflection of motive. The job can be selected as a convenient refuge from the aggressive edge of commercial occupations (e.g. Pearson, 1973, 1975) - a somewhat ironical position from which to counsel clients towards the 'real world'. The work provides some with an emotional bolt hole - within the intensity of client relationships. Unfulfilled desires - maternal, paternal, marital - may channel the choice of client and extent of engagement. A few care less about individual clients than the shape of the society which holds them - yet agency pressures towards one-to-one work significantly frustrates political activity or 'macro' social work. 'Helping others' is a highly qualified slogan in these circumstances, and sometimes a rather hollow one - especially when the balm of social work is perhaps more soothing to the social worker than to the client.

THE CARING SOCIAL WORKER?

Caring for clients may not be a prime motive force amongst all social workers, nevertheless the client setting remains the major arena in which to perform professionally and be judged accordingly - by self, client, peers, superiors, or 'society'. Overt 'uncaring' practice would, therefore, be somewhat self defeating and invite an intrusion into the social worker's much guarded autonomy, as well as threaten career progression. The present study indicates no pervasive insensitivity to client feelings, as suggested by some other writers. Certainly those in or approaching burnout talked disparagingly of their work and clients, but most were not so afflicted. There was generally a compassion for the client in difficulty, although expressed rather more clinically for the disliked client.

The social worker's concern was highlighted in child care decisions, a common difficulty in the profession. Here the anxieties associated with conflicting compassions and interests were only too clear to the worker. The statutory protection of a child at risk, and the embarrassment and sanctions for the social worker in failing to provide such protection, could press or panic the social worker into a decision which would, above all, shield child and self. Despite agency responsibility in these circumstances, extending ultimately to the Director of Social Services, few social workers saw the problem beyond themselves: the spotlight would be on them when disaster struck and their office experiences confirmed this belief. A counterforce to an over-hasty recommendation of a care order was neighbourhood accusations of 'child-stealing', an indictment that few social workers relished. Yet, in a situation charged with tension, conflict and urgency, a social worker, particularly when unsupported, could act in a way that appeared severe, if not ruthless. The situational circumstances partly explain the behaviour, but the action can be a misleading indicator of the social worker's concern for the parties involved. As Tredinnick (1980) reveals in an examination of 160 statutory care cases, social workers are more often than not deeply affected by the dilemmas which face them in trying to meet the conflicting needs of parent and child - and then having to live with unsavoury consequences of their decision.


GOING IT ALONE

The social worker's professionalism, or 'semi professionalism' (see Toren, 1972; Etzione, 1969) finds much of its expression in autonomous, privatised client contact and related decisions. Agency accountability, through supervision, paperwork and resource gatekeepers, blurs this focus. It tends to be seen as far more obstructive than facilitative, generating work rituals which are self-serving. In the present study, some social workers 'played the system' ingeniously to their own ends, learning how best to survive an alien bureaucracy and remain professionally intact. Others, though, had neither appetite nor skill for such a contest and would resent the administrative tangles and fights which drained their energies. Yet should a social worker assert his or her autonomy by avoiding agency demands, and also withdrawing from peer contact, there were costs to bear. Not least of these was a lonely independence, divorced from the emotional and practical support that even the most self-reliant worker could need at times. Furthermore, the organisation had created an apparatus well tuned to its statutory obligations and attendant paperwork. Should the social worker fall short here, vulnerability to organisational sanctions - inspections from higher management, career threats, or even dismissal - markedly increased.

## THE 'TEAM'

The social work team is largely taken for granted as the main organisational unit of practice in the local authority setting, and is similarly conceived in some other social service agencies. Social workers could, and did, talk of their allegiance to, and place within their team, but it was the physical gathering of all members in team meetings which most clearly symbolised the team's unity or disunity of purpose. The latter prevailed. It was consistent with individual definitions of aim and purpose, and the frequent anxieties underlying these, that shared or corporate task activity was unlikely to occur. Any esprit de corps fast gave way to in-fighting, games and ploys, and the ritual of personal agendas would soon swamp the formal agenda. The tension in meetings was overwhelming for some in the present study - they would withdraw psychologically and seek excuses not to attend. Also some staff, such as home help organisers and social work assistants, would regard themselves as marginal members, having to attend meetings which 'weren't for them'. The productive harnessing of all of these forces fell to the team leader. Few seemed able to rise to this, perhaps unenviable task. Indeed, more often than not, the team leader's approach was identified as one of the contributory factors to disharmony in the meeting. In this respect it was not a simple matter of how 'structuring' or otherwise the leader was, as suggested in some of the literature. The difficulties lay in the history of trust and mistrust

between the leader and the group, the leader's ambivalence of role hovering somewhere between a team
manager and a social worker, the skill with which
the leader translated senior management expectations, and the extent to which the leader, unwit-
tingly or otherwise, made demands which transgressed
the social worker's integrity of practice.

There were some social workers who could function
outside the embraces of the team - and were glad to
do so. For them, the formal team meant little more
than an organisational label, equivalent to 'the
office', or 'my place of work'. For others, though,
the team denoted rather more: it characterised a
climate of work - 'friendly', 'supportive', 'fragmented', 'tense' - which comprised an important part
of their feelings about the job, as well as a standard of comparison with other offices and work
places. Yet, for most, the 'real' team emerged from
the shadows and reflections of the formal team.
These were highly valued informal pairings and sub-
groups which cut across and sometimes supplanted the
roles of formal supervision and team meetings. To
varying extents, they met individual's needs for
emotional and task support, as well as helping to
determine their organisational identity - ground
easily trampled upon by remotely controlled organisational change.


BEYOND WORK

A curious omission, or neglect, within the literature concerns the influence of off-the-job factors
on a social worker's stress. This is inconsistent
with what we know about the aetiology of stress, and
certainly does not fit with some of the findings of
the present study. Threat, stress and coping are
intimately related across life experiences. Acute
or chronic home difficulties can substantially
affect a social worker's perception of, and sensitivity to, client and office demands, and managing
this often shifting boundary can be critical in
determining stress. To 'switch off' awareness of
home pressures at work was one form of cognitive
defence which could help a social worker to function
in the job - but not without a reduction in emotional tolerance, perhaps the social worker's most
precious resource. The work/non-work interplay was
sometimes a finely balanced one, and easily upset by

the next difficult client, office squabble, or
crisis demand; and without some appreciation of the
worker's broader life space, the stress reactions
which could ensue would make little sense.


COPING AND SURVIVAL

Social workers are inventive in their stress coping.
The stress and burnout studies reveal many forms of
adaptation to threat and stress, and one can see the
agility of the best copers who, in drawing upon a
range of different resources, create their kit for
survival. The bleaker picture, though, is sharpened
in this study. Many workers are unable to sustain
the defensive/avoidance postures which provide them
with an uneasy, and often temporary, peace. For
example, administrative demands are evaded but eventually become onerously intrusive. Desired work is
carefully protected, only to be threatened in the
next run of work allocation or reorganisation.
Supervisory sessions become progressively more tense
and stilted as mutual suspicions and game playing
run their course. For others, sheer exhaustion and
helplessness attend their failures - such as with
clients who relapse after many months or years of
effort, or have seemingly intractable problems.
Still others find their inadequacies revealed as the
quantity and irregularity of their case load
increase, as crises come and go, and as battles with
key agents inside and outside  the organisation are
lost. And it is at these points that the personal
realities of stress, with its varied psychological
and physical manifestations, begin to threaten the
social worker's minimal survival in the job.

'Minimal survival' is basically a condition of
self where the main contractual requirements of the
job - implicit and explicit - are just about being
met. Where, for example, the social worker's atten-
dance at work is irregular, but sufficient to see
most clients, particularly the statutory cases.
Where essential paperwork is eventually completed,
but other administration is neglected. Where some
supervisory and office meetings are attended, but
many are missed. But, most importantly, where the
quality of performance in all of these areas is
felt, by self and others, to be poor. There is

little feeling of excitement, challenge or creativity in work:   it is a mechanical and generally meaningless process.

A social worker who is not surviving would cease to function sufficiently to manage at this minimal level. This might be a temporary lapse, or a more permanent one where the social worker has to leave the job.   Surviving well would imply a creative and developing approach to the job where enjoyment and challenge are prominent experiences.

Episodic stress could characterise all points on the survival continuum, from those who survive well to those who do not, although the skills of coping (the survival kit) are likely to be more sophisticated and more effectively deployed amongst the good survivors.   The marginal survivors, such as the burned-out workers, are more chronically stressed and are using considerably more defensive energy in attempting to keep their heads just above water.

THE LOCUS OF CHANGE

The present study indicates the scope for change at the level of an individual's workplace realities.   I have assumed that 'out there' characteristics of the organisation and beyond - structures, rules, regulations, procedures, budgets, work schedules - are relevant to stress only when they are 'in here'. And then, in common with much organisational life, especially for certain professionals, work is as much disordered as ordered, and is laced with inconsistency and irrationality. If such be the position, there are some difficulties for the 'top down' changers, or anyone who chooses to tackle stress by revising the shape and purpose of the organisation. To expand this point.

There is no guarantee that executive changes in structures, tasks and responsibilities within a prevailing system will be received and acted upon as intended.   Perhaps the contrary is more likely. Many will fend off the changes, especially if they are imposed, and others will reinterpret them according to their own personal and professional realities.   One may indeed attempt to make a clear statement as to the 'objectives and proper function of social work' (e.g. Stevenson, 1978), but whether this would influence the social worker's <u>experienced</u> ambiguity of purpose, success and meaning in client work, is a moot point. The experienced task might reflect executive intention if the two are closely related - psychologically speaking. Often this is not the case because the creators of objectives (e.g. senior managers) are often organisationally remote from the enactors (e.g. social workers), and subject to different political pressures. Meaningful consultation between them is difficult in such circumstances. It is also doubtful whether any amount of consultation can handle the distinct personal agendas that social workers inject into their role, idiosyncracies which may have an overriding effect on what they feel and do.

The re-defining and re-ordering of objectives will, no doubt, go on. Such acts, however illusory in their quest, can reinforce the belief (to governors and governed) that anarchy is not just round the corner, and that clear means and ends within the job can be determined. Yet these efforts might also be directed towards examining just how enabling existing structures are for social workers, <u>as they perceive them</u>, and their influence on stress and burnout. The present study suggests that the local authority social worker is a professionally skilled, thinking individual, whose actions are partly, and differentially, controlled by organisational mechanisms - supervision, team meetings, resource minders, obligatory paperwork, a hierarchy of responsibility. At worst these seem part of a meaningless, obstructive and stressful game, and at best operate tolerably because of the informal compensatory systems which have evolved. The agency's activities are skewed towards statutory obligations, which give rise to obsessive checking procedures that are rarely infallible, placing considerable authority, but not ultimate responsibility, on the social worker's shoulders. The agency's protection of its front-liners, though, is revealed to be somewhat of a myth - for the social worker in a crisis the buck stops at his or her desk, in that person's view.

Some freedom from this tangle may be possible if the social worker could take personal and legal accountability for his or her actions, along the lines of the probation officer and other 'fuller' professionals. Currently the 'agency' is accountable (symbolised by the social worker being forbidden to sign his or her own letters). The social worker is not directly accountable, in person, to the courts, nor can he or she take personal responsibility for decisions involving, say, compulsory care orders. It is interesting to note that the 1983 Mental Health Act makes provisions to change this, to create a type of social worker, properly trained, to take on such responsibilities. How such individuals will fit and cope within the traditional system will need to be observed, but it does provide one avenue for a clearer status and autonomy for the social worker.

Beyond freedom and autonomy of practice, what the social worker does seem to require is a clear, legitimate and accessible network of resources to call upon for emotional and practical support, a network separate from supervisory structures. This might include independent counselling and psychotherapeutic advice, colleague groups, professional advisors, interlinked training and development activities, and day or residential retreats. The worker could negotiate his or her own package or framework of help to suit ongoing concerns or needs. The stresses of client work could be contained or mollified through such facilities which should be quite free from the imperatives of a work bureaucracy and control. Any further organisation beyond this would need to provide day-to-day clerical and administrative support centred upon serving the social worker in his or her client work - and the flatter, more decentralised, such organisation the better if bureaucratic arthritis is to be avoided.

In respecting the social worker's professionalism, client activity is undertaken in the way the social worker sees fit, and the stresses of this are handled through supportive resources, learned coping, and defences. Yet survival in social work cannot depend solely on 'on demand' resources and incidental learnings. There is an important foundation of pre-job knowledge and skills which currently appears to be missing. Thus social work training requires a clear emphasis on survival in practice, alongside normal professional skills. For the social worker, the two areas are inextricably interlinked. Many of the stress sources and dynamics revealed in this study, and in others, are amenable to teaching and discussion - such as organisational pressures, team politics, the social worker's insti-tutionalisation, client attachments, alienation, the compromising of ideals, the elusiveness of success, and non-work pressures. We are able to address how these affect personal stress, burnout and survival in the job, and strategies for stress management can be explored and rehearsed. This would leave the social worker perhaps a little better equipped for what might lie ahead.

# Bibliography

Adams, J.D., (1978), 'An Action-Research Based OD Intervention', in Burke, W.W. (ed), **The Cutting Edge**, University Associates, La Jolla, California.

Addison, C., (1980), 'Tolerating Stress in Social Work Practice: The Example of a Burns Unit', **British Journal of Social Work**, vol. 10, pp. 341-356.

Argyris, C., (1980), **Inner Contradictions of Rigorous Research**, Academic Press, New York.

Armstrong, K.L., (1979), 'How to Avoid Burnout: A Study of the Relationship Between Burnout and Worker, Organizational and Management Characteristics in Eleven Child Abuse and Neglect Projects', **Child Abuse and Neglect**, vol. 3, pp. 145-149.

Barrett, M.C. and McKelvey, J., (1980), 'Stresses and Strains on the Child Care Worker: Typologies for Assessment', **Child Welfare**, vol. LIX, pp. 277-285.

Birney, R.C., Burdick, H. and Teevan, R.C., (1969), **Fear of Failure**, Van Nostrand-Reinhold, New York.

Bogdan, R. and Taylor, S.J., (1975), **Introduction to Qualitative Research Methods**, Wiley, New York.

Brammer, L. and Shostrom, E. (1968), **Therapeutic Psychology**, Prentice Hall, New Jersey.

Brewer, C. and Lait, J., (1980), **Can Social Work Survive?**, Temple Smith, London.

Carpenter, P., (1977), 'A View of the Client/Worker Encounter', **Smiths College Studies in Social Work**, vol. 47, pp. 167-180.

Cherniss, C., (1980), **Staff Burnout**, Sage, Beverly Hills.

Clark, P.A., (1972), **Action Research and Organizational Change**, Harper and Row, London.

Daley, M.R., (1979), 'Burnout: Smouldering Problems in Protective Services', **Social Work**, vol. 24, pp. 375-379.

Douglas, J.D., (1970), **Understanding Everyday Life**, Aldine, Chicago.

Dunham, J., (1980), 'The Effects of Communication Difficulties on Social Workers', **Social Work Today**, vol. 11, January.

Dunham, J., (1981), 'Resource Checklist to Help You Reduce Tension at Work, **Social Work Today,** vol. 12, March.

Edelwich, J. and Brodsky, A., (1980), **Burn-Out**, Human Sciences, New York.

Egan, G., (1975), **The Skilled Helper**, Brooks/Cole, California.

Eldridge, W., Blostein, S. and Richardson, V., (1983), 'A Multi-Dimensional Model for Assessing Factors Associated with Burnout in Human Service Organizations', **Public Personnel Management**, vol. 12, pp. 314-321.

Etzione, A., (1969), **The Semi-Professions and Their Organization**, Free Press, New York.

Fineman, S., (1979), 'A Psychosocial Model of Stress and its Application to Managerial Unemployment', **Human Relations**, vol. 32, pp. 323-345.

Fineman, S., (1981), 'Funding Research: Practice and Politics', in Reason, P. and Rowan, J., **Human Inquiry**, Wiley, Chichester.

Fineman, S., (1983), **White Collar Unemployment - Impact and Stress**, Wiley, Chichester.

Fineman, S. and McLean, A.J., (1984), ' "Just Tell Me What to Do" - Some Reflections on Running Self-Development Training Programmes', in Cox, C. and Beck, J. (eds), **Management Development: Advances in Practice and Theory**, Wiley, Chichester.

Fineman, S. and Mangham, I.L., (1983), 'Data, Meanings and Creativity: A Preface', **Journal of Management Studies**, vol. 20, pp. 295-300.

French, W.L. and Bell, C.H., (1973), **Organization Development**, Prentice Hall, Englewood Cliffs, New Jersey.

Golembiewski, R.T., (1982), 'Organizational Development (OD) Interventions, Structures, and Policies', in Paine, W.S. (ed), **Job Stress and Burnout**, Sage, Beverly Hills.

Goodman, P.S. and Kurke, L.B., (1982), 'Studies of Change in Organizations: A Status Report', in Goodman, P.S. (ed), **Change in Organizations**, Jossey Bass, San Francisco.

Harrison, R., (1972), 'Role Negotiation: A Tough Minded Approach to Team Development', in Burke, W.W. and Hornstein, H.A. (eds), **The Social Technology of Organization Development**, NTL Learning Resources Corp., Virginia.

Heckhausen, H., (1967), **The Anatomy of Achievement Motivation**, Academic Press, New York.

Herbst, P.G., (1976), **Alternatives to Hierarchies**, Martinus Nijhoff, The Hague.

Huse, E.G., (1980), **Organization Development and Change**, West, St. Paul.

Kerlinger, F., (1973, **Foundations of Behavioral Research**, Rinehart and Winston, New York.

Kadushin, A., (1974), **Child Welfare Services**, Macmillan, New York.

Lewin, K., (1952), **Field Theory in Social Science. Selected Theoretical Papers**, Tavistock, London.

Lewis, H., (1980), 'The Battered Helper', **Child Welfare**, vol. 59, pp. 195-201.

Lofland, J., (1976), **Doing Social Life: The Qualitative Study Human Interaction in Natural Settings**, Wiley, New York.

McNeely, R.L., (1983), 'Organizational Patterns and Work Satisfaction in a Comprehensive Human Service Agency: An Empirical Test', **Human Relations**, vol. 36, pp. 957-972.

Mangham, I.L., (1979), **The Politics of Organizational Change**, Associated Business Press, London.

Mangham, I.L., (1982), 'The Research Enterprise', in Nicholson, N. and Wall, T. (eds), **The Theory and Practice of Organizational Psychology**, Academic Press, London.

Maslach, C., (1978), 'The Client Role in Staff Burnout', **Journal of Social Issues**, vol. 34, pp. 111-124.

Maslach, C., (1982), 'Understanding Burnout: Definitional Issues in Analyzing a Complex Phenomenon', in Paine, W.S. (ed), **Job Stress and Burnout**, Sage, Beverly Hills.

Mattinson, J. and Sinclair, I., (1979), **Mate and Stalemate**, Blackwell, Oxford.

Mawby, R.I., (1979), 'Social Work Under Pressure', **International Social Work**, vol. 22, pp. 47-57.

Mayer, J.E. and Rosenblatt, A., (1975), 'Encounters with Danger. Social Workers in the Ghetto', **Sociology of Work and Occupations**, vol. 2, pp. 227-245.

Niehouse, O.L., (1983), 'The Road to Burnout in the Public Sector', **Supervisory Management**, vol. 23, pp. 22-28.

Paine, W.S., (1982), 'Overview: Burnout Stress Syndromes in the 1980's', in Paine, W.S. (ed), **Job Stress and Burnout,** Sage, Beverly Hills.

Pearson, G., (1973), 'Social Work as the Privatised Solution to Public Ills', **British Journal of Social Work**, vol. 3.

Pearson, G:, (1975), **The Deviant Imagination**, Macmillan, London.

Pettigrew, A.S., (1973), **The Politics of Organizational Decision Making**, Tavistock, London.

Pfeffer, J., (1981), **Power in Organizations,** Pitman, Marchfield, Mass.

Pines, A.P. and Kafry, D., (1978), 'Occupational Tedium in the Social Services', **Hospital and Community Psychiatry,** vol. 29, pp. 233-237.

Pines, A. and Maslach, M., (1978), 'Characteristics of Staff Burnout in Mental Health Settings', **Hospital and Community Psychiatry**, vol. 29, pp. 233-237.

Pines, A.M., Aronson, E. and Kafry, D., (1981), **Burnout,** Free Press, New York.

Prodgers, A., (1979), 'Defences Against Stress in Intake Work', **Social Work Today**, vol. 11, September.

Sandford, N., (1970), 'Whatever Happened to Action Research?', **Journal of Social Issues**, vol. 26.

Satyamurti, C., (1981), **Occupational Survival,** Blackwell, Oxford.

Schein, E. (1969), **Process Consultation: Its Role in Organizational Development**, Addison-Wesley, Reading, Mass.

Shannon, C. and Saleebey, D., (1980), 'Training Child Welfare Workers to Cope with Burnout', **Child Welfare**, vol. LIX, Septem ber-October.

Smith, J., (1978), 'Caring for the Carers', **Community Care**, August.

Stevenson, O., (1978), 'Practice: An Overview', in Stevenson, O. and Parsloe, P. (eds), **Social Service Teams: The Practitioner's View**, H.M.S.O., London.

Stevenson, O. and Parsloe, P. (eds), (1978), **Social Service Teams: The Practitioner's View**, H.M.S.O., London.

Streepy, J., (1981), 'Direct-Service Providers and Burnout', **The Journal of Contemporary Social Work**, June, pp. 352-361.

Sweeney, D., (1981), 'Burnout: Is it Really a Stress Syndrome?', in Paine, W.S. (ed), **Proceedings of the First National Conference on Burnout**, Philadelphia, November.

Taylor-Brown, S., Johnson, K.H., Hunter, K. and Rockowitz, R.J., (1981), 'Stress Identification for Social Workers in Health Care: A Preventative Approach to Burn-Out', **Social Work in Health Care**, vol. 7, pp. 91-100.

Tonnesmann, M., (1979), 'The Human Encounter in the Caring Professions', **Social Work Service**, vol. 21, pp. 34-41.

Torbert, W., (1976), **Creating a Community of Inquiry: Conflict, Collaboration, Transformation**, Wiley, London.

Toren, N., (1972), **Social Work. The Case of a Semi Profession**, Sage, Beverly Hills.

Tredinnick, A., (1980), 'Left Holding the Baby', **Community Care**, April.

Warwick, D.D., (1981), 'Managing the Stress of Organization Development', **Training and Development Journal**, vol. 35, pp. 36-41.

Watson, K.W., (1979), 'Social Work Stress and Personal Belief', **Child Welfare**, vol. 58, pp. 3-12.

Weick, K.E., (1979), **The Social Psychology of Organizing**, Addison-Wesley, Reading, Mass.

Weick, K.E., (1982), 'Management of Organizational Change Among Loosely Coupled Elements', in Goodman, P.S. (ed), **Change in Organizations**, Jossey Bass, San Francisco.

# Index

173